Laughter in Interaction

Laughter in Interaction is an illuminating and lively account of how and why people laugh during conversation. Bringing together twenty-five years of research on the sequential organization of laughter in everyday talk, Glenn analyzes recordings and transcripts to show the finely detailed coordination of human laughter. He demonstrates that its production and placement, relative to talk and other activities, reveal much about its emergent meaning and accomplishments. The book shows how the participants in a conversation move from a single laugh to laughing together, how the matter of "who laughs first" implicates orientation to social activities, and how interactants work out whether laughs are more affiliative or hostile. The final chapter examines the contribution of laughter to sequences of conversational intimacy and play, and to the invocation of gender. Engaging and original, the book shows how this seemingly insignificant part of human communication turns out to play a highly significant role in how people display, respond to, and revise identities and relationships.

PHILLIP GLENN is Associate Professor and Chair at the Department of Organizational and Political Communication, Emerson College. His publications include *Studies in Language and Social Interaction* (co-editor, 2002), *Your Voice and Articulation 4th edition* (co-author, 1998) and *Media '95: Experiences and Expectations Five Years After* (editor, 1996).

Studies in Interactional Sociolinguistics

EDITORS
Paul Drew, Marjorie Harness Goodwin, John J. Gumperz,
Deborah Schiffrin

Laughter in Interaction

PHILLIP GLENN

CAMBRIDGE
UNIVERSITY PRESS

PUBLISHED BY THE PRESS SYNDICATE OF THE UNIVERSITY OF CAMBRIDGE
The Pitt Building, Trumpington Street, Cambridge CB2 1RP, United Kingdom

CAMBRIDGE UNIVERSITY PRESS
The Edinburgh Building, Cambridge, CB2 2RU, UK
40 West 20th Street, New York, NY 10011–4211, USA
477 Williamstown Road, Port Melbourne, VIC 3207, Australia
Ruiz de Alarcón 13, 28014 Madrid, Spain
Dock House, The Waterfront, Cape Town 8001, South Africa

http://www.cambridge.org

© Phillip Glenn 2003

First published 2003

Printed in the United Kingdom at the University Press, Cambridge

Typeface Sabon 10/13 pt.   *System* LaTeX 2_ε [TB]

A catalogue record for this book is available from the British Library

Library of Congress Cataloging in Publication Data
Glenn, Phillip J.
Laughter in interaction / by Phillip Glenn.
  p. cm.
Includes bibliographical references and index.
ISBN 0 521 77206 0
1. Conversation analysis. 2. Laughter. 3. Social interaction. I. Title.
P95.45.G57   2003
302.3′46 – dc21   2002041682

ISBN 0 521 77206 0 hardback

Contents

Figures and tables

Figure

Tables

Acknowledgments

Parts of this book began in my doctoral dissertation from the University of Texas at Austin, completed in 1987. Robert Hopper directed it. He was my mentor, colleague, and friend until his death in 1998, and he remains an influence and inspiration to me. Madeline Maxwell, Joel Sherzer, Mark Knapp, and John Daly guided me as committee members. Gail Jefferson's research appears prominently in this book, and I follow her path with the greatest respect for her work. I've profited from occasional correspondence and talks with her. I continue to learn about the study of talk-in-interaction from many people, particularly Emanuel Schegloff and Anita Pomerantz. Wayne Beach has provided encouragement and rich talks about research. Paul Drew has given enormously helpful and substantive feedback on drafts of this book. Other sources of help, feedback, and encouragement include Eric Kramer, Gene Lerner, Bob Sanders, Kristine Fitch, Jenny Mandelbaum, Curt LeBaron, and Bryan Crow. Colleagues and students at Southern Illinois University at Carbondale provided me a supportive intellectual community during the time I wrote most of this book. Dean Shirley Clay Scott of the College of Liberal Arts at SIUC provided funding so I could take time off from being department chair during Summer 2000 to work on the book. I appreciate the assistance of many fine graduate assistants over the past several years, including Lance Lippert, Liz Gullickson-Tolman, Patreece Boone, Alex Kozin, Stephanie Poole-Martinez, Sam Thomas, Sunita Sunderrajan, and Cade Farmer. Thanks to the staff of Cambridge University Press for being most helpful, especially my editors Andrew Winnard and Lesley Atkin. I've presented parts of this research at the Department of Communication, University of Texas at Austin; Department of Communication, University of

Colorado, Boulder; Department of Communication, University of
Iowa; and School of Communication Studies, San Diego State
University. Each has given me the opportunity to refine my work.
Liliana Cirstea Glenn deserves huge credit for love, support, suste-
nance, critical discussion, and so much more. For these and many
other personal and intellectual influences, I am grateful.

Chapter 3 reworks two previous publications. The multi-party
interaction part appeared in *Western Journal of Speech Communication* (Glenn, 1989). The two-party discussion appeared in *Research on Language and Social Interaction* (Glenn, 1992). Chapter 5
on *laughing at* and *laughing with* is rewritten from an article that
appeared in an edited volume of conversation analytic research
(Glenn, 1995). Chapter 6 draws on an earlier conference paper, co-
authored by Erica Hoffman and Robert Hopper (Glenn, Hoffman,
and Hopper, 1996, March). An earlier version of parts of Chapter 6
appears as a chapter in a book (Glenn, 2003) and had an earlier in-
carnation as a conference paper (Glenn, 2000). The Car Talk from
NPR excerpt (Chapter 6) is used with permission from hosts Tom
and Ray Magliozzi, c 1997 Dewey, Cheetham & Howe, all rights
reserved.

Transcript excerpts used in this book come from a variety of
sources. Many are based on recordings I have collected myself or
others have given me. These are designated by an identification code
that marks collection, tape, and/or page, such as "UTCL AIO," "SIU
JM 99," or "RAH II." I either created these transcripts myself, or I
revised them from originals by someone else. Where a transcript item
is cited from a chapter or article by another author, I have included
its source, and sometimes in those sources the authors provide additional locational data (e.g., GTS:I:1:14, 1965, in Jefferson, 1985,
p. 28). I invite readers to contact me if interested in obtaining copies
of any of my transcripts or recordings.

Finally, I would like to dedicate this book to the family that nur-
tures and sustains my spirit to laugh, especially my mother, Ethel
Chappell Glenn; my uncle, Wallace Chappell; and my wife, Liliana
Cirstea Glenn.

Transcription symbols

Adapted from system developed by Gail Jefferson, printed in J. M. Atkinson and J. Heritage (eds.) (1984) *Structures of social action; studies in conversation analysis* (pp. ix–xvi). Cambridge University Press.

[ ]	brackets indicate overlapping utterances.
=	equal marks indicate contiguous utterances, or continuation of the same utterance to the next line.
(.)	period within parentheses indicates micro pause.
(2.0)	number within parentheses indicates pause of length in approximate seconds.
ye:s	colon indicates stretching of sound it follows.
yes.	period indicates falling intonation.
yes,	comma indicates relatively constant intonation.
yes?	question mark indicates upward intonation.
yes!	exclamation indicates animated tone.
yes-	single dash indicates abrupt sound cutoff.
y<u>es</u>	underlining indicates emphasis.
YES	capital letters indicate increased volume.
°yes°	degree marks indicate decreased volume of materials between.
hhh	h indicates audible aspiration, possibly laughter.
•hhh	raised, preceding period indicates inbreath audible aspiration, possibly laughter.
ye(hh)s	h within parentheses indicate within-speech aspiration, possibly laughter.

((cough))	items within double parentheses indicate some sound or feature of the talk which is not easily transcribable, e.g. "((in falsetto))."
(yes)	parentheses indicate transcriber doubt about hearing of passage.
↑yes	upward arrow indicates rising intonation of sound it precedes.
↓yes	downward arrow indicates falling intonation of sound it precedes.
£yes£	pound signs indicate "smile voice" delivery of materials in between.

Introduction

Those who attempt scholarly works about laughter or humor often begin with an apology responding to one of two sorts of complaints. The first is that laughter is trivial, unimportant, associated with children and with momentary diversions from the more serious, important business of (adult) human life; therefore, it hardly seems worth serious scholarly investigation. The second is that, even if one grants the potential importance of studying laughter, one kills the joy in the subject matter by analyzing something so natural and spontaneous, perhaps akin to dissecting fish in an attempt to understand the way they swim in streams. I will not begin this book by making such apologies. The defenses they might generate, however, are worth noting. Briefly, for those who might wonder, the following assertions underlie this study of human laughter in interaction. In its ability to display affiliation, friendliness, or even intimacy, laughter plays an important role in the creation and maintenance of interpersonal relationships. It can also serve to mock, deride, and belittle others, when it is the laughter of cruelty and triumph. We laugh accompanying and responsive to all sorts of talk and actions: often but not always as a response to humor, but also when we feel nervous or simply when others are laughing. Laughter has been part of the human communicative repertoire for a very long time, probably even predating speech, and our higher primate cousins also enact behaviors that look and sound like laughter and serve similar purposes. It appears to be universal in form and function across diverse human languages and cultures. Plenty of evidence suggests that plenty of laughter provides significant physical and psychological benefits that contribute to individual well-being.

Laughter, then, is important. It is also study-able. Contrary to some popular notions, we humans do not laugh uncontrollably or randomly. Rather, transcription and analysis of everyday interaction reveal that people laugh in systematic, sequentially, and socially organized patterns. Laughing is finely coordinated with speech and with various social activities. Through laughing, and laughing together, we contribute to the ongoing creation, maintenance, and termination of interpersonal relationships. We also display, read, and negotiate identity. In short, the careful study of human laughter reveals much about its forms, functions, and uses, and such study reveals much about human communication in all its facets.

The research reported in this book follows methods of an empirical, inductive, descriptive research tradition known as conversation analysis (CA). With intellectual ancestry in phenomenology, born from the ethnomethodology of Harold Garfinkel and influenced by the micro-sociology of Erving Goffman, CA concerns the description and interpretation of peoples' methods for organizing their social interactions. Conversation analysts study recordings of naturalistic interactions, create detailed transcripts which attend to features of sequential organization, identify particular phenomena, and provide analysis of how those phenomena work situated in local contexts. Within CA research, numerous articles, papers and monographs over the past twenty-five years have described various aspects of the sequential organization of laughter in interaction (Glenn, 1987, 1989, 1989a, 1990, 1992; Glenn, 1995; Glenn, Hoffman, and Hopper, 1996; Haakana 1999; Hopper and Glenn, 1994; Jefferson, n.d., 1972, 1974, and 1979, 1984, 1985, 1994; Jefferson, Sacks, and Schegloff, 1977, 1987; Sacks, 1992, vol. 1, 671–672) . These articles are dispersed among various journals and edited books. One purpose of this book is to provide comprehensive review of CA research on laughter, from the 1970s to the present.

Plan of the book and preview of chapters

Chapter 1 leads to a rationale for a social interactional approach to laughter via a brief critical overview of the diverse writings on the subject. Physical approaches treat laughter as natural, instinctual, common in humans and primates; such approaches feature scientific description of laughter as vocal and visual behavior. Psychological approaches treat laughter as the product of external stimuli plus mental mechanisms and seek to identify variables in both domains. Included here are theories about why we laugh, sometimes framed as what makes humor. Social approaches regard laughter as fundamentally located between people and strive to identify how such factors as presence and behavior of others, role, and context influence laughing. Still, laughter tends to get treated as a passively produced, dependent variable. An alternative view put forward treats people as rule-orienting social beings who actively produce laughter at particular moments in order to accomplish particular ends. Much remains to be learned about how we do laughter in everyday life and how laughter does us. By this (perhaps strange) use of the verb "do" I mean to suggest that people produce laughter, like we do all aspects of communication, in orderly and patterned ways. Furthermore, as we do laughter, it "does" us: laughing contributes to the ongoing creation of meaning, self, relationship, society, and culture. The study of laughter-in-interaction yields surprisingly robust and compelling findings about these processes.

Chapter 2 responds to the call issued in Chapter 1 for a social interactional approach by introducing CA as a research method and some of the initial findings about laughter drawn from close attention to details of recorded and transcribed interactions. In a brief overview I discuss theoretical assumptions and research procedures followed in CA. The transcription of naturally occurring interaction that is central to CA procedures makes available for study the systematic features of laughter. A review of early CA research on laughter, primarily that by Gail Jefferson, presents initial observations and terminology for describing laughter. The chapter closes with a discussion of how laughter coordinates with speech and with other laughter.

The coordination of one person's laughter with another's leads us to a consideration of *shared* laughter in Chapter 3. The sharing of laughter with others indicates affiliation, an alignment of perspectives, and perhaps even celebration. Jefferson first observed that much shared laughter comes about not through simultaneous onset but through a sequence of one person laughing first in a way which invites another to laugh along. First laughs occur within speech or following the completion of an utterance. Recipients respond with laughter, thus accepting the "invitation" and co-initiating shared laughter; with silence, which invites pursuit of shared laughter; or with serious talk on topic, thereby declining the invitation to laugh. Brief laugh particles and smiles sometimes serve as mid-points between accepting and declining a laugh invitation, and data from institutional interactions point to ways in which people orient to certain roles and situations by limiting their laugh responses. Furthermore, in certain contexts a first laugh routinely gets treated not as inviting other to laugh along but as displaying the speaker's orientation towards the talk-in-progress. In these and other ways, the placement of laughs shows sensitivity to the sequential environments in which they occur.

Much of the early CA research on laughter relied on audio recordings as primary data, and claims were limited to aural features. A next section of this chapter extends earlier findings by considering visual cueing of shared laughter. Smiles can operate as milder alternatives to laugh invitations, when they appear in slots where second laughs might occur. Furthermore, smiling and establishing mutual eye gaze can work to create an environment ripe for beginning shared laughter. In these and other ways examination of video materials enriches understandings of laughter in interaction and renders the picture more complex. The final section of this chapter considers how people continue laughing together once they have started. As with beginnings, extensions do not just happen automatically; people must create them, and there are methodical procedures for doing so. These include extending laugh units themselves; extending reference(s) to a single laughable; and extending a shared laughter episode by generating next-in-a-series laughable(s). Through such techniques, a single moment of shared laughter may evolve into a prolonged, communal laughing together.

Chapter 4 raises the question of who laughs first. Laughs generally have a clear referent (the laughable), and ownership or responsibility for the laughable proves a social feature of some importance. A first laugh by the person who also produces the laughable offers quite different interactional possibilities than does first laugh from someone else hearing/perceiving the laughable. The latter situation may involve teasing or laughing *at*. Whether the current speaker laughs first reflects an orientation to the number of parties in the interaction. In two-party shared laughter, commonly the current speaker laughs first. In multi-party instances, shared laughter is more likely to begin with someone else proffering first laugh. Reasons for this and implications of these differences provide the focus for this chapter. The argument is developed that laughing or not laughing, first or following, provide ways for participants to align themselves in respect to the laughable and to each other.

Issues of alignment remain the focus in Chapter 5, as analysis increasingly shifts from central concern with how people organize laughter to what people do through and with the organization of laughter in interaction. Laughter can bring people together, but it can also provide a way for people to show disaffiliation, superiority, or disdain towards others. The terms *laughing with* and *laughing at* reflect these different possibilities. Four keys appear pertinent to how people negotiate whether one's laughter is *with* or *at* another: the nature of the laughable, (who produces) the first laugh, (presence or absence of) a second laugh, and (possible) subsequent talk on topic. Negotiating these matters is emergent and subject to redefinition, however, and the chapter closes with case studies of people transforming a *laughing at* environment to *laughing with*, and vice versa.

The fact that laughter plays a part in displaying affiliation or disaffiliation leads to a broader consideration of its potential contributions to creating, maintaining, and transforming interpersonal relationships and facets of individual identity. Chapter 6 explores how laughter contributes to interactional *intimacy*, treated here not as a static or stable feature of relationship but as emergently displayed at particular moments. The analysis also shows how laughter contributes to *play* in conversation. The treatment of play here draws on frame theories developed by Bateson and Goffman regarding play as a metacommunicative frame created, maintained, and terminated through particular keys, sometimes present and sometimes taken-for-granted. A case study shows how a young woman and man laugh their way through talk which allows them to tease, flirt, play, and suggest (but ultimately back away from) displayed relational intimacy. *Laughing along* implicates participants in activities such as teasing or using improprietous language. Recipients may also *resist* through their laughter. A case study shows how such resistance gets accomplished. Just as laughter provides a resource for working through issues of relationship, it also provides a resource for displaying and negotiating facets of individual identity.

One such facet, gender, provides the focus for a closing section to Chapter 6. A common assumption exists that women laugh more in response to men's laughables than do men to women's. Such a trend gets interpreted in light of claims that women orient more to politeness and do more of the "work" of conversation, whereas men orient more to status and holding the floor (as in joke telling). Empirically demonstrating the relevance of gender (or any other particular feature of context) to the organization of interaction requires documenting participant orientation to it. Evidence for such an orientation may appear in the choice to laugh or not, length and placement of laughs, and more. The attempt to find such a link raises substantive questions about gender and communication and methodological questions about how we may account for the influence of context in talk-in-interaction.

Chapter 7 offers concluding commentary and suggestions for future research. Following review of major findings, I make connections to related research agendas. I close the book with consideration of what "practical applications" might be extractable from the research presented herein.

1

Towards a social interactional approach to laughter

This book is about laughter as a part of everyday human communication. The central focus of subsequent chapters concerns sequential organization of laughter in interaction, what people do with and through laughter, and the ways laughter plays a part in constituting identities and relationships. These topics foreground laughter as communication and as fundamentally social. They represent a shift in emphasis from previous research that has given greater emphasis to its physical, biological, philosophical, and psychological dimensions. Specifically, this book addresses three general questions:

> How do people accomplish laugher in everyday interaction? That is, how is laughter organized, produced, and interpreted?
>
> How do people laugh together? How is shared laughter brought about, maintained, or closed?
>
> What do people accomplish through laughter in interaction?

These questions represent something of a departure from much previous research on laughter. However, they reflect grounding in over twenty-five years of conversation analytic investigations into the sequential organization and interactional workings of everyday laughter, and those materials are reviewed in detail beginning in Chapter 2. In this chapter I provide an overview of some ways laughter has been regarded and studied, thereby positioning this book as building on, and to some extent contrasting with, what has gone before. The familiar but enigmatic phenomenon of laughter has long drawn the fascination and interest of scholars of nearly every academic discipline (for other related reviews, see Monro, 1963; Hertzler, 1970; Goldstein and McGhee, 1972; Holland, 1982;

Morreall, 1983; Zijderveld, 1983; Norrick, 1993; Foot, 1997; and Provine, 2000). Although we tend to think of it as a unitary concept, the term laughter in fact covers a wide variety of behaviors, manifested in different sights and sounds, occasioned by diverse stimuli, and contributing in a multitude of ways to human interaction. We can consider laughter from many different perspectives. It is a physiological process and a perceptual phenomenon. It is universal among humans and probably shared with certain other species, prompting theorizing about its origins and evolutionary functions. It is behavior produced in response to certain stimuli. It is a lived experience involving one's body and emotions. It can make people feel good, and it draws attention for its possible physical and psychic benefits. It is communicative action, influenced by and contributing to social interaction. As a prime indicator of humor or play, it helps us understand what makes something funny, how we signal a playful mood, and what constitutes mirth. As an integral (yet commonly overlooked) part of our communicative repertoire, often accompanying linguistic activity, laughter invites examination of details of its systematic organization and the part it plays in bringing people closer together or pushing them farther apart.

   The Oxford English Dictionary (Murray et al., 1933, p. 103) defines the verb *laugh* this way: "To manifest the combination of bodily phenomena (spasmodic utterance of inarticulate sounds, facial distortion, shaking of the sides, etc.) which forms the instinctive expression of mirth or of the sense of something ludicrous, and which can also be occasioned by certain physical sensations, esp. that produced by tickling." What this definition emphasizes, and what it overlooks, both prove instructive. It invites close attention to physical and psychological dimensions of laughter. The "utterance of inarticulate sounds" locates laughter as vocal behavior but different from speech. Descriptions of the face and body point out that laughter is visual as well as auditory. Use of the word "instinctive" suggests that laughter lies in the domain of automatic responsive behaviors. The phrases "expression of mirth or of sense of something ludicrous" imply consideration of mental causes of laughter and major theories of humor. The last clause reminds us that laughter does not occur solely as a response to humor but can have other causes, tickling being one. Absent from the *OED* definition, however, is an understanding of its social and communicative aspects.

When and where people laugh, how laughter takes on meaning, how it comes to be understood as nervous, hearty, mild, and so forth, how we use laughter to show who we are to each other: all these have provided topics for preliminary investigations in recent years but remain unexplored territory, as yet unreflected in the dictionary definition.

These and other themes are taken up in the following sections. The first section roughly organizes research investigating *how* we laugh. The second concerns *why* we laugh. Third, the section on *social aspects* of laughter pays more attention to ways in which activity, participants, context, and so forth shape human laughter. A final section, "Towards a Social Interactional approach to laughter," locates the approaches taken in this book in light of others reviewed above. CA methods and findings spelled out beginning in Chapter 2 offer new answers to the question of how we laugh, placing greater emphasis on laughter's sequential placement in the stream of human interaction. Subsequent chapters characterizing shared laughter and laughter's interactive accomplishments offer new insights into social aspects of laughter. Finally, exploring how laughter contributes to relationship and identity revisits the "why" questions by examining what people accomplish in and through laughter in interaction.

How we laugh

Research foregrounding the physical processes of laughter provides a major line of answers to the "how" question. Perceptually, laughter consists of a combination of phenomena involving the face, voice, and torso. Francis Bacon (cited in Gregory, 1924, p. 25) wrote: "Laughter causeth a dilation of the mouth and lips; a continued expulsion of the breath, with a loud noise, which maketh the interjection of laughing; shaking of the breasts and sides; running of the eyes with water, if it be violent and continued." Charles Darwin (1872/1955) gave this description:

> The sound of laughter is produced by a deep inspiration followed by short, interrupted, spasmodic contractions of the chest, and especially the diaphragm . . . From the shaking of the body, the head nods to and fro. The lower jaw often quivers up and down, as is likewise the case with some species of baboons, when they are much pleased.
>
> During laughter the mouth is open more or less widely, with the corners drawn much backwards, as well as a little upwards; and the upper lip is somewhat raised. (p. 200)

Visual manifestations of laughter are most noticeable in the face. The mouth opens and the upper lip is raised, partially uncovering the upper front teeth. There is a downward curving of the furrows that extend from the sides of both nostrils to the corners of the mouth. The cheeks puff out on the outer side of the furrows. Creases occur momentarily under the eyes. Prolonged laughter stimulates reflex lacrimation or production in the tear glands, resulting in a "brightening and sparkling of the eye" (Pollio, Mers, and Lucchesi, 1972, p. 212). There is a decreased tendency to maintain visual contact while engaged in laughing. Repeated head movements may occur (Van Hooff, 1972, p. 232; Black, 1984, p. 2995). In its facial appearance, laughter bears close association with smiling, and they often occur together. In the torso, hearty laughter involves involuntary contractions of abdominal muscles, heaving of the chest, and shaking of the sides. An intense laugh may also remove the laugher momentarily from participating in ongoing interaction, as that person may bend over, look down or away, or cover the mouth.

The sounds of laughter, although widely varied, share certain characteristics (see Provine, 2000, pp. 56–63). A minimal laugh sound consists of an explosion of air within speech or freestanding. Freestanding laughs include a number of short, rhythmic syllables, each containing the voiceless, glottal fricative *h*, preceding and/or following either an open-mouthed vowel or a nasal. With the advent of sophisticated recording and sound analysis equipment have come more technical descriptions of human laughter. Provine and Yong (1991) describe a stream of laughter as having a "sonic signature" characterized by four stereotyped features: note structure, note duration, internote interval, and decrescendo. The note structure tends to follow a distinct pattern. It begins with an abrupt, forceful expiration consisting of a "voiceless aspirant of about 200 ms" (milliseconds) (Provine and Yong, 1991, p. 116). The subsequent stream of laughter includes alternating syllables of the voiceless aspirant plus vowel sound, with interval pauses (Black, 1984, pp. 2995–2996). The average duration of one of these syllables is 75 ms. The average internote interval is 210 ms. Peak amplitude tends to be on the initial note followed by a decrescendo (Provine and Yong, 1991, p. 117). Measuring laughs produced under controlled conditions, Mowrer et al. (1987) found a mean duration of an entire laugh to be 1330 ms, and a mean number of syllables in such a laugh to be 7.16.

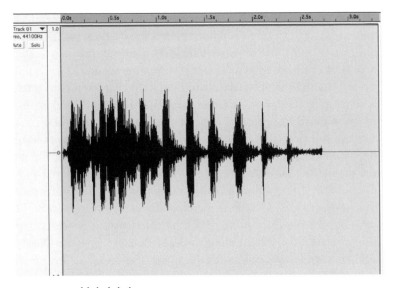

KRISTIN   ₁uhh heh heh
WILSON   ˡihh h<u>e</u>h ↑<u>h</u>he h<u>e</u>h h<u>e</u>h heh heh heh hah hah

Figure 1.1 Picture of a sound image of a stream of laughter. The transcript below (UTCL J2) corresponds to the sound images.

Pollio, Mers, and Lucchesi (1972, p. 216) show that laughs vary in onset latency from laughable, duration of the laugh, and peak amplitude.

The spectrograph image (Figure 1.1) shows sound waves resulting from a stream of laughter produced by two speakers in conversation. The spoken utterance is represented underneath the image. This is not intended to demonstrate a typical laugh, but rather to show visually the pattern of bursts followed by decreased sounds that characterizes lengthy laughs.

The sounds of laughter vary, but less so than, for comparison, speech sounds of any particular language. Their standard features allow for recognition; their variability permits them to do different kinds of interactional work. Such features become relevant for social actors faced with the daily tasks of coherently producing and interpreting laughter. Ironically, as researchers develop greater sophistication in measuring laughter, the descriptions generated move farther away from understanding it as part of the human communicative repertoire. Descriptions arising out of traditions such as ethology and psychology tend to reflect concern with generating context-free descriptions of what humans do. The researcher's eyes and ears are not those of participants who interpret possible laughs in order to be able to take a next turn in interaction. In the quest for objectivity in the positivist tradition, such characterizations tell us something about how laughter is manifested visually and acoustically, but at the expense of understanding these as potentially socially willful, interpretable, and integrated in the stream of joint human conduct. For example, it is interesting to note that the visual manifestations described above resemble those associated with other intense emotional displays or physiological states of distress. This similarity may contribute to ambiguity in how perceivers make sense of someone displaying these characteristics. It suggests that people rely on contextual clues to decide what is or is not hearty laughter versus, say, indigestion or anger. The processes by which such interpretations get worked out tend to get flattened in research that isolates laughs and treats them as discrete phenomena.

Contrast the following two descriptions. The first by Frederick Stearns treats laughter and giggling as objective, physical phenomena: "Giggling differs from laughing by the pitch of phonation which is related to the frequency and location on the continuous scale of sounds and by the accelerated rhythm" (Stearns, 1972, p. 18). The second by Charles Gruner treats laughter as a socially constituted and understood phenomenon; he lists various English synonyms to characterize different ways to laugh:[1]

There is the laughter of rejoicing, exultation, exultancy, delight, joy, elation, gladness, triumph, jubilation. There is laughter which is a signal of mirth or merrymaking or congratulation. There are giggles (all varieties), titters, smirks, grins, sniggerings, chuckles, guffaws, cachinnations. Laughter comes in bursts, fits, peals, shouts, and roars . . . One may cackle with laughter, burst out with it, or split one's sides with it . . . There is sardonic laughter, wry laughter, gay laughter, morose laughter, infectious laughter, and derisive laughter. (Gruner, 1978, p. 41)

This latter perspective more closely approaches understanding laughter as a social phenomenon, produced and understood in situ by participants.

The list above can be interpreted as claiming both that these different types sound different and that laughs differ based on what they are doing at the moments they arise in interaction.

Are the sounds themselves interpretably different for social actors, independent of social context? Patricia Milford (1980) found evidence to support this possibility. She recorded laughs of people responding to four kinds of stimuli: social, tension-release, humor, and tickling. The recorded laughs were analyzed to determine duration, intensity, and mean frequency. She found significant differences between the acoustics of humor/socially stimulated laughs and tension-release/tickle-induced laughs. She also found that listeners could distinguish between these types of laughs based purely on the laughs, without any contextualizing features provided. Thus it seems clear that variations in the physical production of laughter strongly influence interpretations of its meaning. By having subjects judge laughs, Milford moves a step closer to treating laughter as a social rather than purely physiological phenomenon. Still, research treats laughter in isolation, independent of naturalistic social contexts.

Why we laugh

Why do people laugh? Why did this form of communication emerge in our species? Why do we laugh the way we do? What provokes laughter? These and related questions have been the subject of speculation, theory, and experiment in previous research. As a whole, these efforts tend to treat laughter as response to stimulus, whether external or internal or some combination thereof. They have tended not to treat laughter as something people can do systematically, even strategically, integrated with other communicative behaviors.

Cross-cultural research indicates that laughter appears in extremely similar forms across diverse cultures and linguistic groups (see Edmondson, 1987), suggesting its universality. Resemblances between human laughter and the rhythmic, staccato syllables and open-mouthed play displays of certain primates (Loizos, 1967, p. 205; Van Hooff, 1972, p. 235) invite speculation that it has long been in our repertoire of communicative behaviors, perhaps even predating the development of speech (Fry, 1977, p. 24; this relates to Bateson's 1972 theory that an ability to metacommunicate, demonstrated in play, was necessary for language to develop; thus play preceded language). A related issue concerns why the particular sounds and sights that constitute laughter might serve such

evolutionary functions. Darwin offers a theory explaining why the
sounds of laughter might take the form they do as expression of
pleasurable feelings:

> We can see in a vague manner how the utterance of sounds of some kind
> would naturally become associated with a pleasurable state of mind; for
> throughout a large part of the animal kingdom vocal or instrumental sounds
> are employed either as a call or as a charm by one sex for the other. They
> are also employed as the means for a joyful meeting between the parents
> and their offspring, and between the attached members of the same so-
> cial community. But why the sounds which man utters when he is pleased
> have the peculiar reiterated character of laughter we do not know. Nev-
> ertheless we can see that they would naturally be as different as possible
> from the screams or cries of distress; and as in the production of the latter,
> the expirations are prolonged and continuous, with the inspirations short
> and interrupted, so it might perhaps have been expected with the sounds
> uttered from joy, that the expirations would have been short and broken
> with the inspirations prolonged; and this is the case.   (Darwin, 1872/1955,
> p. 205)

Eibl-Eibesfeldt (1989, p. 138) links laughing sights and sounds directly to hostile behavior: "The loud utterance of laughter is derived
from an old pattern behavior of mobbing, in which several group
members threaten a common enemy. Thus it is a special case of aggressive behavior[.]" William Fry (1977) suggests that laughter may
have developed as a means of displaying appeasement to potential
adversaries, thereby defusing possibly threatening situations. Bailey
(1976, pp. 21–23) claims laughter emerged as a "protective device,"
its noise serving to scare off attackers. Gruner (1978, pp. 42–44) attributes its origins to feelings of "sudden glory" – that laughter grew
out of a vocalized cry of triumph in victory after battle. Ludovici
(1932) also takes this position, suggesting that since teeth-baring
often provides a means of warding off an enemy or attaining dominance, laughter following successful combat might be interpreted as
"a claim of superior adaptation." He also poses laughter's role as a
possible alternative to combat. Hayworth (1928, p. 369) offers the
idea that in pre-lingual times, laughter provided a means to signal
group safety or good fortune.

    Whatever its evolutionary origins, laughter appears as an expres-
sive form among diverse human societies, languages, and cultures.
It is both a solitary and a group form of expression:

Laughter is one of the few remaining nonverbal tribal vocalizations. It shares this distinction with crying, humming, roaring (such as a crowd at a sports event), keening, screaming, moaning, and sounds of sexual passion. At least three of the higher primates – man, chimpanzees, and gorillas – exhibit laughter. And, in the case of man, this nonverbal, rhythmic vocalization exists as a major behavior despite the dominance of verbal behavior. (Fry and Allen, 1975, p. 141)

This passage asserts that humans are not alone in having laughter. A number of observers of animal behavior, from Charles Darwin to contemporary ethologists, have noted strong similarities between human and primate laughter. Loizos (1967, p. 205) refers to the "soft guttural staccato exhalations" of primates, resembling human laughs. Van Hooff (1972, p. 235) suggests that human laughter bears phylogenetic proximity to the "relaxed open-mouth display" of primates, which functions in designating accompanying behaviors as play.[2]

The preceding discussion of laughter and smiling suggests these behaviors occur among primates and serve parallel functions as mood signals. Yet some writers differ sharply with this assumption, arguing that laughter is uniquely human. For example, Hertzler (1970, p. 25) asserts that "[t]rue laughter is a phenomenon confined to human beings" and argues that similar behaviors occurring in animals and infants be termed "elementary laughter." Stearns (1972, p. 1) and Askenasy (1987, p. 317) assert that only humans laugh. The evidence from ethological research, mentioned above, clearly refutes such a position. It is more defensible, perhaps, to assert that only humans possess the cognitive sophistication to laugh at jokes, themselves, irony in situations, or word-play. However, laughter as a repetitive sound-pattern and as a facial display to show amusement or friendliness appears at least in chimpanzees and gorillas.

In its facial appearance, laughter bears close association with smiling, and they often occur together. Both can show pleasure or amusement, and both may occur in response to a common stimulus. Some researchers argue that laughter and smiling differ only in degree of intensity; others see them as distinct, although related, phenomena (see Berlyne, 1969, p. 798). Drawing on anthropological evidence, Van Hooff (1972, p. 234) classifies smiles and laughs along a two-dimensional continuum. On one dimension, increased baring of the teeth reflects increasingly non-hostile or friendly attitude.

On the other, increased mouth opening and vocalization accompany increased playfulness. At one extreme, a broad smile can indicate a highly friendly attitude but not necessarily a high degree of playfulness; at the other, an open-mouthed laugh can show a high degree of playfulness, but not necessarily a friendly attitude. Van Hooff suggests that while in primates these facial expressions have relatively distinct features and meanings, they have grown intertwined in the repertoire of human expressions such that their distinctions are largely blurred (Van Hooff, 1972, pp. 235–236). From quasi-experimental psychological investigations, Pollio, Mers, and Lucchesi (1972, p. 213) rank order four reactions to humor stimulus: no response, smile, laugh, and explosive laugh. This ordering suggests laughter as the next-higher level of response along a continuum. Chapman concludes that, "Laughter and smiling probably have different phylogenetic origins, but they clearly converge functionally as non-verbal expressions of humour appreciation" (Chapman, 1976, p. 157). In summary, both expressions can display friendliness and sociability. Laughter is associated more with aggression, dominance, or hostility; smiling is associated more with submissive friendliness. They often co-occur as displays of amusement, although smiling generally marks a milder response.

In the individual, as in the species (see p. 19), laughter predates speech. Infants begin laughing generally about the third or fourth month of life (Stearns, 1972, pp. 47–48). This initial laughter appears stimulated primarily by bodily sensations such as comfort and well-being. Laughter in response to social cues, such as familiar faces and sounds, develops next; laughter in response to tickling does not appear until several months later. Smiling precedes laughter: infants in the first week after birth will smile during REM sleep; by the end of the first month, they usually begin to smile in response to external stimuli (Camras, Malatesta, and Izard, 1991, p. 81). As the child develops, laughs increase in frequency relative to smiles. Although smiling occurs so early in life, researchers have been reluctant to link it with the emotion of happiness for children less than three months of age (Camras, Malatesta, and Izard, 1991, p. 80). Rather, it may be that the infant produces the facial expression, gets a response from others around, and learns, gradually, how that expression gets associated with certain feeling states. Infants first begin to laugh within infant–caregiver interactions anywhere from ten to twenty-one weeks of age. Laugh onset is sudden and dramatic, and once it appears it becomes frequent. Fogel et al. (1997) report different forms of infant laughter they term comment, chuckle, rhythmical, and squeal. As children grow, social factors provoking and moderating laughter become increasingly important. Development brings greater dissociation between the behaviors of laughing and smiling and pure emotions. Differential emotions theory (Camras, Malatesta, and Izard, 1991, pp. 74–75) holds that basic emotions have distinct neural, expressive, and experiential components. In infancy, expressions of these are instinctive. With development they become more restricted and controlled. Thus the child's cognitive and communicative development should accompany an increased ability to produce laughter, not only as direct expression of pleasure or amusement, but also for social reasons. Furthermore, with development comes the ability to modify, exaggerate, mask, or fake laughter, and to recognize these variations in others. Children do not seem as inclined as adults to laugh primarily in response to humorous stimuli, at least in controlled conditions. Summarizing research literature, Foot and Chapman (1976, p. 190) concluded that "laughter is rarely elicited from children unless there is some form of social stimulation accompanying the more obvious laughter-provoking stimuli." Higher frequency of laughs correlates with higher scores on intelligence tests for children, and individual differences in frequency of laughs increases with age.

In this section emphasis has been on laughter as a physical process that is a natural part of the human expressive repertoire. Descriptions of how laughter looks and sounds serve to bring to conscious awareness the bases for perceptions that normally are taken for granted. They lead to consideration of how laughter is both like and different from other bodily processes and communicative displays. Approaches grounded in ethology and anthropology conceptualize laughter as natural, instinctive, ancient in the human repertoire (perhaps predating speech), shared with other animal species, and serving important evolutionary functions. In research on infants and children, emphasis is on development of emotions; laughter and smiling, if studied, tend to appear as indices of feelings such as pleasure or amusement. The emotion–behavior link is considered very strong early in life and increasingly susceptible to other influences as the child develops. However valid this may be as a model of development, it clearly encourages thinking of human laughter as directly linking to and prompted by emotions, as uncontrollable, and as originating in the individual rather than in the interaction. Such research fundamentally operates from a stimulus–response theory of laughter, leaving little room for conceptualizing it as communicative.

Another line of research on laughter, deserving mention due to its current popularity, is less about why we laugh than why we *should* laugh. Many people advocate active pursuit of opportunities for laughter in the belief that it is good for individual health and well-being. Laughter and humor have long been thought important for biological survival, and the absence of them thought to impair health (Berlyne, 1969). The physiological features of hearty laughter have healthful benefits, like aerobic exercise. Strong, mirthful laughter disrupts normal respiratory cycles (Fry, 1977, p. 23), and this increases respiration, muscular use, and heart rate. It stimulates the cardiovascular system, the sympathetic nervous system, hypothalamic–pituitary–adrenal gland production, and production of alertness hormones called catecholamines. These release endorphins, the natural pain killing enzymes that enhance blood flow, reduce inflammation, and contribute to relaxation and a sense of well-being (Robinson, 1983, p. 118; Black, 1984, p. 2996). It causes skeletal muscle contractions. Following prolonged laughter, muscles may remain flaccid and pulse rate elevated (Black, 1984, p. 2996). These responses underlie medical findings about the physiological and psychological benefits of laughter. Yoshino et al. (1996) report positive effects of mirthful laughter on patients with rheumatoid arthritis, who showed significant changes in mood, degree of pain, and various laboratory measures of endorphins. In one famous and well-documented case, Norman Cousins (1979) gave much of the credit for his recovery from a degenerative spine disease to laughing, which he deliberately induced by systematic, regular exposure to humorous materials. Reports by Cousins and others have helped spawn a large popular movement advocating the importance of laughter, a sense of humor, and a spirit of playfulness for individual well-being.[3]

The question of why people laugh has long prompted theorizing and inquiry for philosophers and other scholars. Major theorists sometimes treat this question as synonymous with "What makes something funny?" or "What causes humor?" Conflating these questions implicitly assumes that finding something funny leads necessarily to laughing, and that laughing necessarily is provoked (only) by finding something funny. Setting this limitation aside for the moment, we can appreciate how various theories of humor help pave the way for studying laughter in interaction.

The *superiority/hostility* theory suggests that people laugh when comparing themselves to others and finding themselves stronger, more successful, or at some advantage. This feeling may occur in competitive situations when an individual experiences success over another, or when an individual perceives the other as showing weakness or undergoing misfortune. These situations invoke the speculation (discussed earlier) that laughter evolved from snarls and cries of triumph over a defeated adversary. Superiority theory acknowledges that laughter can carry a hostile or competitive element to it. This is the laughter of the winner in a sports match, the evil villain on stage, or the wit who successfully one-ups adversaries in public. Similarly, perceiving the weaknesses or misfortunes of others enables the laugher to feel superior. Much humor is based on this principle. Slapstick comedy derives its power from the delight audiences feel at seeing someone else suffer the social embarrassment of slipping on a banana peel or getting a pie in the face. Adults enjoying children's errors may laugh while feeling that they have gone beyond such mistakes. Jokes that disparage others draw on the superiority motivation. Henri Bergson argued that humans recognize that the adaptive posture is superior to the inflexible one and thus adaptive, intelligent creatures will laugh at instances of rigidity or mechanical reactions in others. The superiority/hostility theory does not always lead to comforting conclusions about the human species, for it acknowledges our capacity not only to react to the misfortune of others with cruel callousness, but even to help bring about such misfortune, and find it laughable. Clearly, when we feel superior or hostile to others we do not always laugh or feel like laughing. We may also react with hatred, pity, or indifference. Specifying under what conditions superiority leads to the humor response remains an interesting challenge.

The theory of *incongruity* suggests that laughing results from experiencing the unexpected, from a perceived inconsistency between what one believes will happen or should happen and what actually occurs. The incongruity principle is at work when one sees or hears something absurdly out of context or place, such as a bowling ball in a refrigerator. Children's humor, word play, surrealist and dadaist art, and theatre of the absurd all draw on incongruity for ludic effect. Comedy often relies on depicting persons acting, speaking, or being treated unthinkingly, for this violates our taken-for-granted assumptions that people should and will be mindful of themselves and each other. The incongruity between expectations and actuality, between the mechanical and the adaptive, motivates the laughter. This presents an alternative explanation for why we find an unthinking human response funny. Superiority theory claims we laugh at others because this makes us feel better about ourselves; incongruity theory explains laughter as resulting from perceiving the unthinking response as out of place for its situation.

Incongruity may also be understood temporally as a rupture of expectations of what is to come next (Weeks, 1987). Immanuel Kant wrote of laughter resulting from a "strained expectation being suddenly reduced to nothing" (1790/1952, p. 199). Comic timing, according to Jacques Derrida (in Weeks, 1987), sets up, not a static condition, but a crescendo, which then is disrupted when the outcome is "nothing." Many jokes operate on this premise: the set-up creates expectations, or a trajectory, for what is to follow; the punch line shifts frames and delivers "nothing." Joke theories generally rely upon understanding the punch line as shifting frames. Victor Raskin's (1985) semantic theory of humor suggests that if a text is to succeed as a joke, it must carry two different and even opposing scripts (akin to frames). Oppositions are characterized in such terms as sexual/non-sexual, real/not real, or normal/abnormal. Similarly, Arthur Koestler's "bisociation" (1964) theory posits that the humor experience involves a sudden shift between, or combination of, different interpretive frames. The set-up creates one frame of reality or interpretation. The punch line achieves its humorous effect by suddenly shifting to another, equally coherent, but competing frame. For example, here is a joke I heard recently:

A blond enters a library, walks up to the clerk at the desk, and says brightly "I'd like a burger and fries, please." The clerk, admonishing, replies, "Sir, this is a *library*." "Oh" says the blond, who then immediately whispers, "I'd like a burger and fries, please."

This joke's effectiveness relies upon leading the hearer to one set of expectations, then suddenly supplying another set. The first involves a person (the blond) who is so stupid that he[4] does not recognize a library as what it is and treats it as a fast-food place where one would order a burger and fries, and the clerk who corrects him by pointing out that this is a library. The shift in frames lies in the realization that the correction does not work. The stupid person, even more stupidly, persists in ordering a burger and fries, but now does so quietly. He has taken the librarian's correction as referring, not to his ordering food, but to his speaking volume. The bisociative shift can occur because of the ambiguity in the librarian's correction. Merely to say "This is a library" makes available to the other that the context requires *some* kind of adaptation, but does not make explicit what that adaptation should be. The stupid blond chooses a trivial self-correction (and, perhaps not incidentally, one stereotypically associated with librarians – shushing people) but persists in the greater stupidity of trying to order fast food in a library.

The term "bisociation" emphasizes the separation between the two frames. However, it is important to recognize that humor also requires maintaining some coherence between the two. Otherwise, one simply has two unconnected ideas (Mulkay, 1988, p. 31). Mulkay (1988, pp. 32–35) argues that incongruity theories rely upon an assumption that cognition in the humorous mode operates by the same principles as in the "serious" mode. In the serious, it is assumed, one prime interpretive frame at a time operates; if we perceive a second one, we will work to sort out the situation. When humor is offered, we are to shift from a first to a second. In contrast to this thinking, Mulkay claims that in the humorous mode we do maintain mutually contradictory frames of interpretation. In developing this argument he connects to Bateson's (1972) theory that play presents an inherently paradoxical message requiring both serious and non-serious interpretation.

Incongruity theories represent an important advancement in recognizing the sudden shift and resulting surprise that often provoke a feeling of humor and thus laughter. Like magicians' acts, effective jokes work by leading us to one expectation, suddenly to provide us with another different outcome. Such theories, however, do not cover all instances of humor or laughter. They do not explain why some incongruities seem humorous while others do not. They rely on the questionable assumption, also applied to serious discourse, that we can only entertain one coherent frame at a time. In fact, humor often relies on sustaining two or more frames simultaneously. Furthermore, these theories are based on considering jokes in isolation from how they are told and responded to in interaction. They assume that laughter operates only as the manifest response of the psychological experiencing of humor.

The *relief* theory posits that people laugh upon realizing that a threat is no longer a threat or upon being freed of some psychological burden. Horror films sometimes create moments of false terror: the creaking door turns out to be only that, nothing more. At such a moment, when it is clear that the tension was unwarranted, audience members will laugh. People getting off a roller coaster at an amusement park will laugh. Laughter may come when one escapes a near accident or expects but does not get some bad news. In these kinds of situations, so the theory goes, laughing provides a safety valve to let out pent-up tensions. Sigmund Freud developed the tension-release theory of laughter consistent with his model of the mind as a storehouse of psychic energy. He argued that considerable psychic energy must be employed to maintain inhibitions. Such inhibitions suddenly get relaxed when one hears an aggressive or erotic joke. Laughter provides a way to release the built-up tensions (Freud, 1938, pp. 734–735). Koestler (1964, pp. 53–60) connects incongruity to release notions by claiming that laughter is the body's automatic reflex response to the experience of bisociation. Why the experiencing of humor would result in the peculiar facial, bodily, and vocal responses that characterize laughter remains a puzzle. Koestler explains these by invoking the claim that humor inherently involves aggression and hostility, to which the body responds, instinctively, with arousal. The arousal builds up tensions which then get released through a channel of least resistance: in the face, voice, and torso, manifested as laughter.

None of these three general theories – superiority/hostility, incongruity, or relief – has gained widespread acceptance as a general explanation of the humor response. We do laugh at times because we feel superior, but this is not always the case. We do sometimes laugh when we perceive incongruity, or when some tension has been released. However, one can readily think of humorous instances that cannot adequately be explained by any one of these theories. Humor may be better understood as a complex response to stimuli – internal and external – combining elements of superiority, incongruity, or release. Contemporary writers have attempted to incorporate all of these causes into a broader theory of laughter. Further developing a Freudian theory of the mind, Daniel Berlyne (1969, pp. 838–840) places importance on the need for an optimal level of arousal to maintain psychic equilibrium. He argues that either an increased or a decreased level of arousal in stimulus materials can motivate laughter, the laughter providing a means to restore the optimal arousal level. Feelings of superiority, incongruity, or relief might contribute to increased or decreased arousal, and this motivates laughter. Another contemporary theory is based primarily in the incongruity notion but attempts to incorporate the other two. John Morreall (1983, p. 39) puts forward the simple claim: "Laughter results from a pleasant psychological shift." It is viewed as the outward manifestation of a change in sensory, affective, perceptual, or cognitive state. The change must be sudden, too sudden for the mind to adjust otherwise, in order to generate the tension released through laughter. The shift must be "pleasant," which would rule out such experiences as being frightened or learning of bad news. Forwarding primarily the incongruity notion, this theory also takes into account feelings of superiority and release, both treated as "pleasant" mental shifts. Morreall's theory includes non-humorous laughter such as that done in response to tickling or embarrassment. It acknowledges that superiority and tension release may be present but are not necessary to laughter.

Morreall's theory seeks a more comprehensive account for laughter by explaining its occurrence as a response both to humor and to other situations and causes. It is clear that much human laughter occurs independent of humorous stimuli, or at least its connection to a humor source often is not direct or linear. Descriptors such as "nervous," "insincere," or "wicked" applied to laughter imply something more than simple perception of humor. Monro (1963, pp. 20–82) lists the following as "non-humorous stimuli": (a) tickling, (b) laughing-gas, (c) nervousness, (d) relief after a strain, (e) "laughing it off," (f) joy, (g) play, (h) make-believe, and (i) contests. Foot (1977, pp. 271–275) lists the following as "functions" of laughter: humorous laughter, social laughter, ignorance laughter, evasion laughter, apologetic laughter, anxiety laughter, derision laughter, and joyous laughter. However one cuts the laughter pie, it is evident that it does much more than merely respond to humor.

Tickling is an odd case. As any reader who has been tickled can attest, tickling is not funny, though it is a laughing matter. Tickling-induced laughter seems unrelated to any perception of humorous-ness. Rather, it is responsive to social factors involving potential physical threat by a dominant other (Yoon, 1997). Another odd sit-uation involves rare cases in which excessive, forced, or epileptic laughter occurs. These have been explained as due to pathologies or abnormalities of the brain or central nervous system (Duchowny, 1983). Leopold (1977) reports on the case of a man who began to laugh when making certain eye movements in intense illumination; a large extramedullary brainstem tumor was found to be respon-sible. Black (1984) reports laughter as having been observed as a symptom of brain damage. These cases aside, human laughter has a decidedly social basis to it.

Recent psychological research moves away from the temptation to treat laughter simplistically as response to humor and thus to im-ply a causal, stimulus–response relationship from humorous event to perception of humor to laughter. Foot and Chapman (1976, pp. 188–191) differentiate "humorous" from "social" and other kinds of laughs which are not prompted by humorous stimuli, al-though they caution that these should not be considered mutually exclusive possibilities. Laughter is so inconsistently associated with humor that experimental psychologists have abandoned using it as a reliable indicator that the subject perceives something as funny (Berlyne, 1969, p. 796; LaFrance, 1983, p. 2). Furthermore, there is growing recognition that as perceptions of pleasure or humor can provoke laughter, so laughing can lead to perceptions of pleasure or humor. The responsive signal can prompt individuals to experi-ence the inner states that usually are thought to precede or cause that signal. Morreall (1983, p. 55) refers to this as a "two-way causality" of laughter with certain psychological states.

An alternative approach to classifying stimuli as humorous or non-humorous begins by describing those remarks, actions, or situ-ations in response to which people actually laugh. Pollio and Edgerly (1976, p. 219), summarizing their own and prior research covering a fifty-year span, indicate five general situations in which college students laugh, according to self-report data. The most commonly reported situation features such events as "Wisecracks, put-downs, clever remarks, jokes, stupidity of others." Other situations for laughter include: "Happy mood in general," "Physical actions and antics of other people," "Incongruous incidents and situations," and "Formally funny materials – plays, radio programmes, movies, etc." Martha Cox (1982) recorded and analyzed statements "said with a laugh" in naturalistic settings. She found laughs most often in such statements as boasts, challenges, humorous utterances, and emotionally laden utterances. Laughs occurred less often in supportive statements, requests for or offers of information, or observations about the group. The possibility that laughter alone (independent of humorous stimulus) begets laughter was tested by Provine (1992). Students listened to a laugh box and the researcher noted whether or not they laughed in response to it. Most of them did the first time. Over nine more successive times, fewer and fewer subjects laughed. By the tenth, most reported finding it annoying. Provine concluded that laughter's power to provoke laughter is limited absent any further humorous stimuli (see discussion below on extending laughter, pp. 73–74).

The research reviewed so far shows progression towards more complex treatments of the question of why people laugh, from evolutionary-based theories about laughter's role in adaptation, to theories about what makes something funny, to comprehensive theories taking into account non-humorous causes, to studies documenting when people actually laugh. There appears to be growing acknowledgment that many factors, internal and external, affect or stimulate laughter. Treating it solely as a response to a stimulus produces only incomplete understandings. Certainly there are situations in which feeling triumphant, noticing an absurdity, or experiencing tension release may prompt laughter. Tickling, embarrassment, or other non-humorous stimuli may prompt laughing. At times it is faked, produced strategically, or done simply because others are doing the same. When we shift from studying it as behavior to studying it as communication, then linking it to some particular causal stimulus recedes in favor of characterizing how its meaning gets constituted jointly by laughers and hearers. The studies reviewed in the following section deal with social and environmental factors, thus moving us a step closer to a comprehensive account of laughter as it occurs in human interaction.

Social aspects

Laughter involves physiological and psychological processes. However, it is clear that laughter has strong social dimensions too. Much can be learned by investigating social factors that influence laughter and, in turn, how laughter works in social situations, between individuals, and within and among groups. The recognition that laughter does not provide a direct barometer of perceived humor opens up questions of what other factors might influence its occurrence and what else it might be doing. Prominent among factors influencing laughter are social variables such as whether others are present, whether others are laughing, who they are, what is going on between participants, what the laughable is about, and so forth. Osborne and Chapman (1977) found striking evidence for the importance of the presence of others in influencing laughter. Subjects exposed to the same humor stimulus materials showed enormous differences in the amount of laughter, depending upon variations in the social environment. Subjects paired with a cooperative confederate, who laughed when subjects did and was generally responsive, provided by far the greatest amount of laughter. Subjects exposed to the same humor stimulus materials who were alone laughed less often. However, subjects paired with a nonresponsive confederate (one who did not laugh) produced only a few laughs of short duration. Brown, Brown, and Ramos (1981) found that college students laughed most often when someone else in the room with them was laughing too. In contrast to the Osborne and Chapman study, they found that students laughed least when alone compared to when with a non-laughing co-participant. Freedman and Perlick (1979) report that neither the presence of a laughing, smiling confederate, nor crowding influenced subjects' amount of laughing; however, they did find an interaction effect such that the two factors together increased subject laughter. Despite some contradictory outcomes, these studies all suggest that people are more likely to laugh when others around are laughing.[5]

This social facilitation of laughter prompts the use of live studio audiences or "canned laughter" in the radio and television industries (Rosenbaum, 1978). Several studies have investigated the impact of laugh tracks or the sounds of audience laughter on subjects' laughing behavior and perceptions of the funniness of the humor materials. Chapman (1976, p. 156) reported that dubbed laughter significantly increased the amount of laughter displayed by subjects; however, it did not significantly increase their subsequent ratings of the perceived funniness or cleverness of the humorous materials. Martin and Gray (1996) studied subjects listening alone to a recorded radio comedy show. Those who heard it with live audience laughter rated the program significantly funnier and more enjoyable. They also laughed and smiled more, but not to a degree achieving statistical significance. Neuendorf and Fennell (1988) found that students viewing a video accompanied by canned laughter laughed more but did not rate the program as funnier. Although results are not consistent, in general, people laugh more often in the presence of both laugh tracks and live co-viewers laughing. However, neither laugh tracks nor co-present laughing audience members tend to enhance viewers' perceptions of the humorousness of stimulus materials (Neuendorf and Fennell, 1988). There may well be more substantive findings from proprietary research conducted within the entertainment industry that have not appeared in scholarly or popular sources. Producers have persisted over many decades in providing canned or live audience laughter accompanying television comedies on the assumption that this enhances the experience for viewers.

Laughter is influenced not only by the presence or absence of others but also by who those others are. Several researchers claim that women laugh more than men in a variety of social circumstances. These claims receive critical attention in Chapter 6. Summarizing a number of studies of emotional expression (often, but not always, laughter), Wagner and Lee (1999, pp. 263–265) identify two factors that distinguish facilitation of expression from inhibition of expression. First is the role of the other person. If that person is participating alongside the subject, affect display is facilitated; if that person is observing, inhibition tends to occur. Second is relationship: facilitation is more likely to occur when the co-participant is a friend, classmate, or familiar other; when the other is unfamiliar, inhibition more likely occurs. In a naturalistic study of medical teams, Rose Coser (1960) reported that subordinates laughed more at the humorous remarks of superiors than vice versa. It may be that the subordinate (at least in some situations) felt more compelled to laugh at the superior's humorous remarks. An approach

that analyzes laughing behavior as a product of relationship or role
tends to treat communication as static by under-representing the importance of the message being conveyed and the actions being done.
For example, whether a subordinate laughs less than a superior is not
simply a factor of these social roles but reflects what is going on at
moments when laughter might be relevant. Provine (2000, p. 40) reports from studying more than 1200 conversations that in a majority
of instances, laughter was not directly responsive to humor. Often
it accompanied, rather than responded to, humorous utterances;
other times it seemed more related to something else such as politeness or sociability. This research moves us closer to understanding
laughter as communication by regarding what it is doing socially
rather than how it may be linked to some stimulus or inner state.

A fundamental shift towards acknowledging laughter's social
workings is to treat it not solely as responding to humor (thus that
the humor stands independently as such, pre-existing the laughter)
but rather as marking (and thereby helping constitute) its referent
as humorous or playful. Prominent in this line of thinking are frame
theories of Gregory Bateson and colleagues, further developed by
Erving Goffman (1974) among others. Bateson argued that in order
for people or animals to engage in play (which requires being able to
distinguish serious from playful sequences), they must be capable of
exchanging the metacommunicative message "this is play" (Bateson,
1972, pp. 177–193). Framing markers do not alone accomplish creating a playful context; they propose it, but co-participants must
ratify it. In an earlier study (Glenn and Knapp, 1987) Mark Knapp
and I found laughter to be one of the primary frame markers between adults shifting into playfulness. The laugh metamessage may
come from the person who produces the laughable or from someone
else. For example, a speaker may offer a teasing or joking comment
then laugh to make clear that it is meant, and should be taken,
playfully. Likewise, the recipient of some action or utterance may
laugh to show willingness to treat it as play (O'Donnell-Trujillo and
Adams, 1983, pp. 179–184). The metacommunicative function of
laughter is not simply responsive but also constitutive of the context
(Zijderveld, 1983, p. 34). One may laugh not only to ratify an
ongoing comic frame, but also to help bring one about (consider
situations in which people laugh to try to cover up or deal with
embarrassment).

Knowing that laughter displays playful treatment of its referent, participants in interactions may laugh as a means of displaying a certain inner state, or observers may use the presence of laughter to infer the mental state of its producer. Schenkein (1972) suggests that a laugh can show not only that the hearer understands and appreciates a prior laughable, but also displays that the hearer possesses the necessary background knowledge to appreciate it. Similarly, Sacks (1974) shows how recipients' laughter at completion of a joke demonstrates that they "got" the joke, jokes being "understanding tests" for recipients. Falk and Hill (1992) note that in psychological counseling sessions, client laughter may indicate a "desirable" shift in self-concept or otherwise signal mental change associated with heightened experiencing, emotional flooding, or catharsis. Furthermore, they argue that client laughter may express a positive counseling relationship and itself may lead to increased warmth, acceptance, intimacy, and reduction of emotional distance between therapist and client.

As this suggests, laughter proves important socially as a means to show affiliation with others. To laugh when someone else has done something humorous, laughed first, or otherwise indicated a nonserious orientation provides a way to display like-mindedness. Similarly, one may laugh first in order to provide co-participant(s) the opportunity to do the same. Schenkein suggests that laughs

are one of the ways persons can go about proffering or displaying affiliations with one another in the course of some conversation-in-progress. That some second-speaker *heheh* can be heard to support some intendedly nonserious first-speaker's utterance reveals on its occurrence a coincidence of thought, attitude, sense of humor, and the like.   (Schenkein, 1972, p. 371)

This affiliative social function of laughter involves not only a display of mutual understanding, but also mutual closeness or affinity (Hertzler, 1970, pp. 93–97). These are analytically distinguishable notions: one may agree with someone else on some proposition or claim yet not affiliate in treating it humorously. Laughter allows for both possibilities. However, laughter does not necessarily show affiliation or like-mindedness; how it may do so, and in what kinds of environments, are issues taken up in later chapters. Jefferson, Sacks, and Schegloff (1987) show how speakers utilize shared laughter in displaying affiliation and remedying possible interactional improprieties. Their analysis, reviewed in detail in Chapter 6, reveals how participants may display a subtle array of responses from outright rejection to passive acceptance to outright affiliation with improprieties. Laughter plays a prominent role in such sequences.

Because of its ability to show (and produce) affiliation, laughter proves particularly useful in situations of embarrassment, discomfort, or anxiety. Ragan (1990) showed how patients and nurse practitioners routinely use humor and laughter to help get through awkward moments in gynecological exams. Emerson (1973) documented hospital patients employing humorous references to enable them to talk with medical staff about uncomfortable or taboo topics. Mallett and A'Hern (1996) demonstrate laughter's routine occurrence during patient–caregiver interactions in which patients dealing with renal failure must face anxiety related to painful injections and to learning new procedures and machinery. In these and countless other situations, laughter helps people get through socially difficult moments.

One of laughter's most important features lies in its shared nature: that it is produced primarily in the presence of and for the benefit of other persons. In fact, laughter can be "infectious" in an interaction, beginning with one or a few persons and engulfing all present. Shared laughter serves some important functions (below summarized from Hertzler, 1970, pp. 93–98). It provides, at least temporarily, a group unity or awareness, a psychic connection of all the laughers. It can be induced as a means of displaying this group togetherness. It allows for the expression and maintenance of group values and standards, via the subjects and situations to which it refers. It can boost morale and ease internal hostilities or differences. Laughing at people or things external to the group can strengthen boundaries, solidifying members in their group identity against outsiders. The importance of shared laughter is lost in studies that treat laughing exclusively or primarily as the product of the individual mind, or which rely on methods that test the laughing response in isolated individual subjects.

As pointed to in the earlier discussion of superiority/hostility theories, laughter may also contribute to interactional *disaffiliation*. Laughing at someone may demonstrate lack of sympathy, consideration, or alignment. Laughter may hurt and may contribute to feelings of hostility or embarrassment. The same laughter that promotes in-group solidarity may be done at the expense of outsiders, thus accomplishing simultaneously both affiliation and disaffiliation (for example, see Basso's 1979 study of Western Apache speakers making fun of white Americans). More deeply, it may contribute to perpetuating negative attitudes, stereotypes, and temptations to denigrate or dismiss individuals or entire groups of people. These two outcomes viewed together – bonding people while disaffiliating them from others – make laughter potentially a powerful and even subversive social tool. Bakhtin (1968) writes of laughter as a means for lower classes and those in less-powerful positions to challenge the social order by making objects of derision out of those in power and the rituals and rules that maintain existing power relationships. A newspaper editorial (Wright, 1990) notes that the student conduct code of one major US university prohibits "inappropriately directed laughter" on campus. It is because of these capacities that laughter sometimes is considered dangerous, requiring moderation and an ethical grounding.

Towards a social interactional approach

It is possible to detect in the research traditions reviewed above a gradual progression towards treating laughter as first and foremost located in and responsive to social interaction. Mulkay eloquently makes the call for the kind of research this book attempts to provide:

> If laughter *is* more than a mere reflex response to environmental cues, if it *does* contribute systematically to the sign language of the humorous mode and is employed in subtle ways to communicate about the meaning of the ongoing interaction, techniques must be found to investigate the fine detail of laughter in natural settings. We must find a research perspective that not only allows for the possibility that social actors methodically employ laughter as an interactional resource, but also treats such laughter as a topic for careful investigation.   (Mulkay, 1988, p. 110)

It is apparent that laughter defies easy description or explanation. It has what Black (1984, p. 2995) calls a "chameleon nature." The similarity of laughter across various languages and cultures (and among our primate cousins) suggests its universality and long history in human communication. However, there is considerable variation in what laughter looks and sounds like. Its causes appear to be many, from tickling to finding something funny to covering a faux pas. It can be understood as simple reflex, as social nicety, or as malicious insult. It is strongly social, in that its occurrence, form, and meaning are shaped deeply by the presence of others, roles, relationships, activities, and other contextual features. It appears early in life and quickly develops in complexity. Laughing can make us physically and mentally healthier, and yet it can be cruel and cause great distress.

The research reviewed under the first section of this chapter emphasizes laughter as physical action and physiological process. In answering the question, "How do people laugh?" this research treats the phenomenon as natural, instinctual, and out of our control; as a pure expression of emotion; and as the same throughout cultures and circumstances. Research methods used tend to treat people, not as rule-engaging social actors, but as animals whose actions may be described in neutral, objective language. Laughs get described in isolation from their naturally occurring contexts. Descriptions tend to favor dramatic, extended, hearty laughs, at the expense of the (probably more common) small, subtle, conversational laughs that pepper peoples' talk so pervasively that it is difficult even to notice them.

In contrast to these choices, the research presented beginning in the next chapter focuses on production and interpretation of laughter as intentional social action. "Intentional" here is used in the phenomenological sense, not to suggest conscious awareness or motive, but rather a guided doing with ascribable, accountable purposes. Research issues concern when, where, and in what ways people organize, produce, respond to, and interpret laughter as part of the ongoing stream of interaction. Laughter is regarded not as involuntary reflex or instinct but rather as controllable, systematic, and precisely placed. The emphasis in this research is more on laughter in everyday talk (both casual conversation and institutional interaction) than on that produced by audiences in public or mass communication events. Preference is given to methods producing more naturalistic data rather than data generated in laboratory environments or under somewhat artificial circumstances.

As shown in some of the research reviewed above, the question "Why do people laugh?" has actually served in past research as a means of exploring what makes something funny. This fascinating question has led to intricate theorizing about the mechanisms at work in humor. Superiority, incongruity, relief, and "pleasant psychological shift" theories provide insights into the triggers and reactions that provoke a sense of the humorous that so often triggers laughter. Over-reliance on these theories risks assuming that laughter necessarily is caused by humor, when that is often (perhaps a majority of the time) not the case. Rather, the quest to understand the causes of laughter leads to examining both humorous and non-humorous stimuli. Even this approach, however, unduly limits laughter to a subservient role as response to stimulus. Laughter can serve to create a feeling of humor, it can be faked, it can occur before or during its referent, and it can be induced simply by other laughter. A complete account of laughter as communicative action requires shifting from cause–effect terms that treat people as passive or involuntary creatures to a vocabulary that treats people as willful social actors.

Social approaches reviewed above invite consideration of when, where, with whom, and by whom laughter occurs, while acknowledging that we cannot fully understand it absent its peopled contexts. From this literature comes interest in role and contextual variables influencing the presence or absence of laughter and interest in how it contributes to affiliation, disaffiliation, identity, relationship, and more. The fundamental question shifts from "Why do people laugh?" to "What are people doing when they laugh?" Emphasis is placed on co-construction of sequences, interactions, understandings, and meanings. In such a conception we move away from the simple assumption that laughter follows humor, to a mutual constitution model that suggests that the occurrence of laughter marks its referent (usually retrospectively) as laughable – and, potentially, as humorous. Funniness becomes understood not as an inherent property of a message, or the internal state of a social being, but rather as a jointly negotiated communicative accomplishment. In summarizing and presenting the research that follows I minimize claims about psychological or emotional states of persons laughing. Rather, my focus remains on what people display to each other and accomplish in and through their laughter. The move to empirical documentation of findings evident in the social approaches represents a step forward in the scientific study of laughter in human life. However, findings reported at the aggregate level cannot show how laughter works in particular circumstances. Hereafter, I will rely primarily

on showing detailed transcriptions of recorded interactions as a basis for showing the fine-grained details of actual laugh moments.
Counter to some earlier writings that dismiss laughter as uncontrollable, I begin with an assumption that it has orderly, regular
production and placement features, and I provide evidence of these.
As an antidote to the detached descriptions of laughter that discount
social beings' lived experiences of it, a CA grounding guides interest
in the perspectives of the actors. Further countering any notion that
it works as a pure mood display, I will show that the meaning(s) of
any particular bit of laughter can only be understood by characterizing the actions it accomplishes – and that requires characterizing
the local, sequential environments in which it occurs. Crucial to this
process is interpreting how participants in the interaction themselves
produce and interpret laughter. This ethnomethodological emphasis (explained more fully in the next chapter) moves away from
searching for a comprehensive theory of laughter. Rather, the task is
to account for what laughter does as part of concrete, particular
instances; from these, more generalizable accounts may be built
inductively. The passage from Mulkay cited at the beginning of this
section calls for a method that allows for careful investigation of
the sequential organization and interactional workings of laughter.
For an answer to this call I now turn (as did Mulkay) to conversation analysis, beginning with the research of Gail Jefferson and
colleagues.

2

Conversation analysis and the study of laughter

The preceding chapter ends with a call for research devoted to characterizing patterns of actual human laughter occurring in everyday interactions. Such a research focus is consistent with (and motivated by) the phenomenological, descriptive tradition known as conversation analysis (CA). In this chapter I introduce the study of laughter in interaction through two major parts. First, I review the theoretical assumptions, research agendas, and methods that characterize CA. The second major part of this chapter consists of a review of CA research that provides initial findings and a vocabulary for analyzing laughter in interaction. An emphasis on describing the sequential organization of everyday talk at a highly detailed level leads to remarkable insights about the communicative workings of laughter; this chapter is intended to lay the groundwork for summarizing such research.

The theoretical underpinnings and procedures of CA are thoroughly described elsewhere (see, for example, Levinson, 1983; Atkinson and Heritage, 1984, pp. 1–15; Psathas, 1995; ten Have, 1999). Reflecting its ethnomethodological orientation, CA starts from an assumption that people organize their interactions with each other in systematic, describable ways. The overarching purpose of research is to describe peoples' methods (thus the label ethnomethodology) for "doing" everyday life. Conversation analysts study recordings and transcripts of interactions that are (to the extent possible) naturalistic, rather than those contrived by researchers in order to control such features as settings, topics, or relationships. CA research starts from an assumption that talk is orderly and that this order may inhere in the smallest details, so that no feature may be dismissed a priori or assumed to be irrelevant. Consistent with an ethnomethodological perspective, CA researchers attempt to minimize arbitrarily imposing analysts' categories, presumptions, or world views on the talk. Rather, specified phenomena should reflect participant perspectives, as evidenced in the talk. Utterances, turns at talk, and individual actions provide such evidence, for they are thoroughly interactive creations through which participants display to each other (and negotiate) their ongoing interpretations of the talk-in-progress.

The name "conversation analysis" is misleadingly limited, for data come from, and findings apply to, a wide range of interactions, not just conversation. More formally, the term "conversation" refers to a specified speech-exchange system characterized by a particular set of practices for organizing turns at talk (Sacks, Schegloff, and Jefferson, 1974). However, public speeches, business meetings, interviews, and many other kinds of interactions have been, and may profitably be, studied through the methods of CA. More recently, researchers have referred to this tradition as the study of "talk-in-interaction" (Psathas, 1995, p. 2). Nevertheless, CA remains widely known as a term connoting the coherent set of assumptions and research efforts which inform this book. The term CA also provides a point of contrast with discourse analysis. Although some advocate using discourse analysis as an umbrella term for all approaches to the study of language in use (Tracy, 1998), I endorse Levinson's (1983) use of the two terms to distinguish CA as unique in assumptions and procedures. In particular, the insistence on studying only actual interaction and on specifying participants' procedures and orientations mark CA as a distinct research enterprise.

Recordings serve as primary data for CA research. Sociologist Harvey Sacks and his colleagues, Emanuel Schegloff and Gail Jefferson, took an early interest in talk as a locus of activities concerned with creating and maintaining social structure in everyday life. Sacks (1984, p. 22) made the simple move of tape recording and transcribing talk, not, as he noted, out of any particular theoretical or empirical interest in talk itself, but as a way to study practices through which people provide order to their lives together. The desire in CA is to remain as close as possible to studying actual interaction. A recording already is one level of abstraction removed from events themselves, but it is closer to them than surveys, diaries, or other types of data researchers use to study communication.

Early on in their work, Sacks and his colleagues recognized the importance of attending not only to words but also to other features noticeable in audio recordings. From its inception, CA as a research enterprise has included the study of nonverbal as well as verbal phenomena. When working with audio recordings, analysis must be limited to sound, particularly to voice and speech. With more recent advent of high quality, inexpensive video equipment, many contemporary CA studies attend to visual as well as auditory details of interaction.

Working with recordings involves repeated listening, transcription, and analysis. These are not so much discrete steps as they are cyclical, recursive, and intertwined activities. However, transcription often precedes identification and explication of phenomena of interest; the repeated listening it demands helps bring the researcher into intimate familiarity with the data in ways that facilitate discovery. The widely used transcription system developed by Gail Jefferson invites attention to timing, sequence, sound emphasis, pronunciational variation, silence, and non-speech sounds (see Transcription symbols at the beginning of this book pp. xi–xii; for fuller explanations, see Heritage and Atkinson, 1984, pp. ix–xvi; or Psathas, 1995, pp. 70–78). In creating an initial transcript the researcher attempts to capture as much detail as possible, because when transcribing, one cannot reasonably know what will turn out to be important. For example, to make a transcript of talk showing only words uttered and not the silences between words would forward, however implicitly, a theoretical assumption that silence is unimportant to whatever is being studied. Working with both recordings and transcripts of talk offers distinct advantages over working with only one or the other, or relying primarily on recollection, interview, or other more reductive forms of data. Researchers can listen and view repeatedly, noticing details that might otherwise be missed; researchers also can share findings, transcripts, and recordings with other researchers, thereby providing a reliability check on claims (Sacks, 1984, p. 26).

Transcription precedes but also accompanies close description and analysis. In the early stages analytic work proceeds in an open-ended, "unmotivated" manner (Sacks, 1984, p. 27). The researcher may start from the beginning of the recording, or select any passage of interest, to examine more closely. Often small groups of researchers conduct exploratory investigations in data sessions by listening repeatedly to a fragment of recording (perhaps thirty seconds' to five minutes' worth), examining the transcript, and discussing the fragment in detail. Description never becomes complete but, in a hermeneutic fashion, researchers may return to the same materials again and again to discover new and different observables. Eventually, however, analysis moves to more systematic levels. Perhaps the most common procedure is to identify an instance of a phenomenon, then search for additional examples of it. This process, conducted reflexively with continual revision of the class of objects, leads to a collection of instances of a single structural feature of interaction which recurs across interactions and situations. CA researchers neither assume universality of phenomena nor presume specified limits in ways that reflect a priori assumptions about how certain variables (e.g., gender or culture) shape talk. Rather, generalizability remains an open issue. A second common analytic move is to develop a comprehensive account of a single (often lengthier) instance of talk in which several phenomena combine to create a larger structure or social activity.

Analysis proceeds inductively, building general claims from particular instances. Evidence rests on descriptions of particular instances, which are shown in research reports (and, where possible, accompanied by audio or video excerpts). Claims of a recurrent pattern do not rest on frequency or statistical probability but on demonstration in examples and explication of the practices, orientations, rules, competencies, expectations, etc., which participants display in their conduct. Accompanying such fundamental research processes, some CA researchers provide descriptive statistics, while others argue for strong limitations on the use of them (Schegloff, 1993). All would agree, however, that the primary analytic task is not to count but to show the workings of phenomena in particular instances. In this book, I will from time to time provide frequency counts of occurrences of something or other: who is more likely to initiate shared laughter, whether patients laugh more than doctors, or whether women laugh more than men. Some of these are from my own research and some from other research on laughter. In all such cases, numerical distributions open doors to the possibilities of interactional phenomena, but they themselves are not the phenomena. Finding a statistical trend is not an endpoint of research but provides cause for examination of details of particular instances. This is consistent with CA's continual push to understand features of talk as they unfold in particular situations by and for particular people. We do not live our lives in statistical trends but one moment at a time. Claiming a pattern across cases does not help explain the particular instance, unless evidence appears that participants in that instance orient to the regularity. Furthermore, if the researcher does provide a count, there needs to be some justification that the items being counted may hold some procedural relevance for participants. For example, Schegloff (1993, pp. 103–104) critiques a study that counts "laughs per minute" as a measure of sociability. Although such a standardized metric allows easy comparison across (potentially large numbers of) cases, it stands far removed from peoples' sequential, time-bound experiences of laughing and responding to laughter. As Schegloff aptly puts it, "People do not laugh per minute." Thus, in Chapter 4 when I report counts of when current speaker or someone else initiates shared laughter, I do so based on evidence that interactants treat these options as consequential to producing and interpreting talk.

CA began in sociology but now appears in many disciplines concerned with understanding what humans do. In the discipline of communication, CA has emerged as a widely practiced qualitative method. The communication discipline has long roots in the study of speech from rhetorical and performative perspectives. In the latter half of the twentieth century, it grew into a popular and eclectic field encompassing artistic, humanistic, and social scientific approaches. Given the communication field's central concern with messages and their effects, and with associated phenomena such as how human relationships are constituted through communication, CA provides a natural fit. CA, discourse analysis, ethnography of communication, and sociolinguistic research recently have contributed to an emerging sub-discipline within communication known as language and social interaction (see review by LeBaron, Mandelbaum, and Glenn, 2003).

CA research reports may go beyond characterizing a single instance or a collection of instances of some phenomenon to connect analysis to wider theoretical, conceptual, or methodological issues. The organization of the rest of this book reflects such an emerging emphasis. Earlier chapters primarily present sequential phenomena. Later chapters show how these sequential phenomena play a part in such issues as how intimacy gets displayed in interpersonal relationships and how people orient to gender in interaction.

The data for this book come from a variety of English-language interactions, primarily recorded in the USA and Great Britain. The settings include both personal and institutional environments. Length of interactions ranges from less than one minute to more than one hour. They contain as few as two participants and as many as eight. Relationships of speakers range from intimate to workplace to near-strangers. Individual speakers in these recordings vary by age, race, education, socioeconomic status, and sex. Dates of recording range from the mid-1970s to the late 1990s. On all of these dimensions, I made some attempt to include a variety of materials, but I made no attempt to sample in any systematic way. This is because at this point we have no valid empirical or theoretical basis for sampling individuals or situations relevant to the study of the organization of laughter in interaction. Without clear specification of the population of variables, systematic sampling is premature and might well lead to a kind of Type 1 error, claiming the naturalistic presence of phenomena that are in fact the researchers' inadvertent constructions. However, Chapter 6 considers as an explicit issue whether the gender (or sex) of participants may be directly relevant to the organization and workings of interactional laughter.

The data are naturalistic in that no attempt was made to control how people talk or what they talk about on the recordings. In most cases, people were asked simply to turn on recorders when they would be talking anyway. The recorded interactions are not completely naturally occurring (meaning "free of researcher influence"; see Bavelas' (1995) intriguing deconstruction of the natural–artificial data distinction). Observing (even subtly recording) inevitably has some influence on data, however slight it may be. Despite this limitation, the recordings obtained provide a workable basis for investigating sequential organization and interactional workings of laughter. The laughter people do when they know a recorder is not present does not seem to vary fundamentally or systematically from other laughs (other than the most obvious fake laughs). In many social situations, we orient to being over-heard, monitored, and perhaps even judged by our laughter. In this sense, all social laughs are to some extent influenced by the observer's paradox. Unless we are alone, we are always subject to scrutiny, and our actions display our awareness of this.

None of the participants in these recordings knew that their laughter would be studied. At most, they would have been informed that the recording would be used for research on interaction or in-terpersonal communication. All participants in private interactions gave consent, and opportunities were provided for participants to withdraw if they so chose. I collected some of these recordings my-self; more often, they come from research libraries of recordings, particularly those housed at the University of Texas at Austin and Southern Illinois University Carbondale.

Beginning with an interest in laughter, I selected passages in which people were laughing. These generally are not difficult to identify. Some interactions contain almost no laughter whatsoever; others are so rife with it that scarcely a few seconds pass without more laughter. I made collections of laugh instances, always transcribing several seconds preceding and following the laughs. As research progressed, collections were defined more by phenomena of interest than by the simple presence of laughter. One instance of laughter may serve to illustrate more than one phenomenon and thus may be included in more than one collection.

The rest of this book features claims about laughter in interaction emerging from my research and that of other CA researchers. They are presented as an integrated whole. Demonstration of findings proceeds with heavy reliance on exemplars to support claims. Some exemplars are cited from other CA researchers; often, however, I will provide instances from my data to demonstrate others' findings. This is done intentionally to test and extend the generalizability of earlier claims. Consistent with the analytic induction (Znaniecki, 1934) impulses of CA, attempt is made to come to terms with not only the "typical" cases fitting a general pattern, but also "deviant" cases which seem to run counter to prevailing trends.

A first step in presenting these claims is to introduce some early CA findings about laughter, from research conducted primarily by Gail Jefferson and her colleagues. In addition to intriguing findings,

Jefferson's research provides a vocabulary and way of characterizing laughter within interaction that opens up possibilities for analyses developed in succeeding chapters.

Laughter in talk: initial observations

Some transcriptions of human interaction simply note the occurrence of laughter, such as the following:

(Davies, 1985, p. 134)

1	ED	I'll pay for it.
2	JOYCE	No, I already got it.
3	ED	You shouldn't pay for my coffee.
4	JOYCE	Oh, that's OK . . . You're worth every penny.
5	ED	(laughs) I see your opinion of me has gone up.
6	JOYCE	Not really. I'm coming back later to take 15 cents out again.
7	BOTH	(laugh)

This is consistent with everyday practices of reporting laughter: it is more "normal" to say, e.g., "he laughed," than to say, e.g., "he went 'heh heh hee'." The first CA transcripts followed this pattern. Early on, however, CA researchers became aware of the possible insights to be gained from not only *noting* the occurrence of laughter but also actually *transcribing* the sounds of laughter. By doing so, the transcriber creates a visual analog to the sounds of laughter, inviting readers to notice in print, patterns that occur in interaction. Transcription and analysis of actual conversations allow one to examine laughter-in-use as it occurs: provided for interactively, often shared, and embedded in the sequential context of other conversational activities. People orient not simply to the presence or absence of laughter in conversation, but to its length, placement, acoustic shape, and coordination with other bits of talk. Transcribing laughter rather than simply noting its occurrence in some record of an interaction provides a helpful tool for the analyst seeking to understand laughter as a social phenomenon.

Jefferson (1985) develops this argument in an article demonstrating how full transcription of laugh particles and analysis of their sequential placement contribute to a richer understanding of the role of laughter in talk than would otherwise be possible. First she shows one of her earlier transcripts of an instance of talk, in which an utterance is transcribed this way:

(GTS:I:1:14, 1965, in Jefferson, 1985, p. 28)

LOUISE   ((through bubbling laughter)) Playing with
                his organ yeah I thought the same thing!

The descriptor "through bubbling laughter" limits analysis in at least two ways: it modifies the entire utterance, thus neglecting the possibility that laughter appears only in portions; and the verb "bubbling" suggests that laughter works intrusively, perhaps uncontrollably, into the talk. Using a more detailed system, Jefferson re-transcribed the utterance as follows:

(GTS:I::2:33:r2, 1977, in Jefferson, 1985, p. 29)

LOUISE   heh huh •hh PLAYN(h)W(h)IZ O̲(h)R'N y̲a:h
                I̲ thought the same

Louise laughs preceding and during the phrase "playing with his organ" (which she produces as a mis-hearing, with obscene implications, of another speaker saying "play with his orchids"). Jefferson notes that there is a systematic basis to laughing during the obscenity. By doing so, Louise marks it and invites hearers to make sense of it. The fact that she immediately discontinues laughing and speaks points to how precisely speakers place laughter, even during a moment of raucous merriment. Without detailed transcription of laughter itself, it would be difficult to notice such phenomena.

From slight chuckles to mirthful guffaws, laughter is organized, with systematic sound-production features to which both laughers and other participants orient in the coordination of their interactions. Individual laugh particles appear within a word, between words, or freestanding and independent of words. Laughter from one individual may extend over a number of syllables. Within such a "stream," shifts in volume or position of mouth may occur. Laughter may occupy part of a turn at talk, may occur in spaces between turns, or may constitute a turn itself, with features marking its winding down. In this section, I will discuss these features and introduce vocabulary that helps us describe laughter-in-interaction.

Jefferson's transcription system reflects how participants organize interaction into turns (see Sacks, Schegloff, and Jefferson, 1974). Speakers project turn completion, or what Sacks, Schegloff, and Jefferson (1974, p. 703) characterize as a *transition relevance place* (TRP) where speaker change might occur. Projecting turn completion allows other participants to prepare to take a next turn, helping achieve close coordination of interaction. A stream of laughter (Jefferson, Sacks, and Schegloff, 1977, p. 4), consisting of several discrete particles or syllables produced by one speaker, can appear as part of an utterance containing speech; it can also stand by itself as a turn at talk. A stream of laughter which stands as a full turn (appearing without talk, with a TRP) may be described as an *N-Part Laugh Unit* (Jefferson, Sacks, and Schegloff, 1977, pp. 6–7), with the "N-Part" referring to the number of syllables or particles.

When laughter ends a turn at talk (whether the turn has consisted solely of laughter or included other activities), certain features routinely mark its nearing completion (Jefferson, Sacks, and Schegloff, 1987, p. 155, esp. footnote 2). These include an inbreath laugh particle (indicated by a raised period preceding the sound) and decreased volume (indicated by degree symbols surrounding the sound). Both appear in succession in the excerpt below. Jeanette complains about the coming of fall, and Alice aligns with this attitude by saying it makes her want to cry. Jeanette laughs, ending with an inbreath particle:

(SIUC JC, 1992)

```
1   ALICE       ↑Okay so it's fall Jeanette.
2   JEANETTE    I know. I hate that.
3   A           Makes me wanna ⌈c r y :
4   J                          ⌊huh huh heh heh hnh (.) •uhhh
```

Alice doesn't laugh, but produces a next complaint. Jeanette's next laugh includes three particles, then a fourth at diminished volume:

```
5   A           I hate it when that happens,
6   J           uhhh huh huh °huh°
7               (0.5)
8   A           The sun goes away:.
```

Through and upon the occurrence of such markers, speakers orient to and deal with the possibility of speaker change. In the preceding passage, Alice resumes speech after Jeanette's inbreath laugh particle:

| 4 | J | huh huh heh heh hnh (.) •uhhh |
| 5 | A | I hate it when that happens, |

The inbreath marks this as a moment at which not only speaker transition but cessation of laughter can occur, and in fact does occur in this instance. However, the inbreath laugh does not *necessarily* terminate laughter; more may follow (Jefferson, Sacks, and Schegloff, n.d., p. 54). This involves renewing laughter, which is discussed in Chapter 4.

Let's look more closely at the laughter itself in the passage above. Jeanette's first laugh consists of five syllables, a brief pause, then an inbreath laugh particle.

| 4 | J | huh huh heh heh hnh (.) •uhhh |

There is a shift between the second and third syllables, marked on the transcript by the change in medial vowel from u to e. The fifth syllable sounds closed-mouth and nasal. These outbreath syllables cease, and she vocalizes an inbreath after a brief pause. This six-part laugh unit appears on its own line on the transcript, indicating that it may constitute a turn at talk that achieves possible completion (and thus signal transition relevance).

Jeanette's second laugh, like the preceding one, constitutes a turn at talk. It is a four-part laugh unit in which the fourth syllable drops in volume, signaling possible completion. Because of this marker of transition relevance, the following pause is placed on a separate line on the transcript, indicating that either speaker might self-select to speak next.

| 6 | J | uhhh huh huh °huh° |

Transcription of such features aids the analyst and reader in noticing the fine-grained coordination of laugh units, inbreaths, and termination of shared laughter that these speakers produce.

The laughs shown above are lengthy and freestanding. Some laugh particles appear only as the briefest of aspirations, often embedded within a word.

(UTCL A20a)

    MELODY   •h I can't even remember l<u>a</u>st w<u>ee</u>kend.h
                (0.9)
    ELLEN   You c(<u>h</u>)a:nt?
    MELODY   Unh unh.

Others may accompany speech, appearing at multiple points in talk:

(UTCL D8a)

    LOU   I'm sor-I was-I'm eating right now
              huh huh I had to st<u>o</u>p. °huh-huh° •e<u>u</u>h
              This's LouAnne. huh hu-hih °hh°

Laughs vary in acoustic content, although the range of sounds that people would treat as possible laughter is finite. The prototypical laugh particle is a syllable consisting of aspirated "h" sound plus a vowel. Variance occurs in whether the aspiration precedes and/or follows the vowel and what vowel sound appears. A more open-mouthed laugh may be transcribed as:

(CDII:76)

    MATT   En here c<u>o</u>mes this ↑g<u>u</u>⌈(h)u(h)<u>y</u>,
    NINA   ⌊HAA ↑HAA Haa=
              =H⌈A <u>h</u> <u>a</u> ⌈ha ha ha⌉ ↑•<u>uhh</u> •uhh
    MATT   ⌊on the ⌈wr<u>o</u>ng ↑<u>la</u>:⌋ne.like y<u>ou</u>:.⌋

A more closed-mouth laugh, but still partly open, may be shown as

(SIUC Stan and Dave)

80   DAVE   Put a ↑l<u>ea</u>sh on that thing and leave it in the
81   back yard with a big bowl of food and water.=
82   STAN   =hh hih heh heh °huh huh°=

A laugh with mouth completely closed may be represented with a nasal letter in the vowel position:

(CDII:77)

    NINA   That wz crazy. nhh hn.

Within a single laugh stream of more than one syllable, the acoustic shape may change, from open to closed or closed to open. In the following example, Cara produces three relatively open-mouthed laugh particles (shown as "eh ↑hih hih"), then shifts to closed-mouth, nasal particles (shown as "hn ↑hn hn"), then ends the laugh stream with an inbreath:

(UTCL D8a)

529	RICK	An' then I'm gonna go:un to a movie. °hh hh°
530		(.)
531	CARA	Gunna gone to a movie?
532	RICK	Gonna go:ne to a mov(h)₍ie.
533	CARA	⌊eh↑hih hih
533a		hn ↑hn hn •hhh

Sometimes a marked change in volume or tempo occurs during a stream of laughter. Ed's laughter (lines 79–80) begins with two relatively closed syllables (i.e., a chuckle). After a brief pause, the laughter shifts to open-mouthed with increased volume. This continues for another nine syllables:

(UTCL J1)

71	ED	Wha' does Tara mean by that,
72		(1.1)
73	ED	She b- what' she say in?
74	CARLIN	uh Tara?
75		(0.7)
76	CARLIN	Where is Tara.
77	CARLIN	What a resemblance.
78		(0.5)
79	ED	heh heh (.) HUH-HAH! (.) HAH ↑HAH
80		HAH ₍HAH HAH HUH HUH
81	JAN	⌊ih-hih
82	WILSON	°↑That's rude°

Jefferson, Sacks and Schegloff (1977, p. 9) call this shift "Stepping Up." It displays recognition of some change of understanding for the laugher. In this way, its function may be understood as parallel to the particle "Oh" which may display a "change of state" in the speaker (Heritage, 1984).

Laughter in relation to talk; laughables

Utilizing the features of individual laughs described above we can begin to characterize some ways that laughter coordinates with other activities. Conversationalists regularly face the ongoing task of interpreting actions and utterances and displaying interpretations in producing mutually intelligible social action. The kinds of cues available for interpreting laughter differ in interactionally significant ways from those for speech. Unlike speech, laughter ". . . is not a linguistic construction but an acoustic one, with no readily apparent semantic or syntactic features" (O'Donnell-Trujillo and Adams, 1983, p. 175). Laughing conveys meaning, but that meaning does not arise from its status as a member of a verbal, linguistic code. Nor does its meaning derive from syntax (placement in relation to other words in phrases, clauses, and sentences) in the same way that, for instance, a noun may be understood as subject of a sentence by its placement relative to a predicate. The placement of laughter, however, does matter. In this sense, laughter is *indexical*; it is heard as referring to something, and hearers will seek out its referent (Jefferson, Sacks, and Schegloff, 1977, p. 12).

Sequential placement provides a key clue to identifying laughter's referent (and thus, its meaning). When laughter can be heard as referring to talk, commonly that talk occurs immediately preceding the laugh (Schenkein, 1972, p. 365). While laughs routinely follow completion of a prior laughable utterance, they also routinely appear at an earlier *recognition point* at which the laughable nature of the utterance-in-progress becomes evident (Jefferson, 1974, p. 7). Laughing at a recognition point can display quick understanding of the laughable; it can also ensure prompt speaker transition with no gap, gaps constituting possible evidence of the failure of a laughable. In general, "(l)aughs are very locally responsive – if done on the completion of some utterance they affiliate to last utterance and if done within some utterance they affiliate to its current state of development" (Sacks, 1974, p. 348).

Placement of a laugh relative to its laughable displays precisely what the referent, or laughable is, typically via placement concurrent with or immediately following that object (though it may also refer forward, anticipating or framing an upcoming laughable). It displays to co-participants that the person laughing takes that referent as laughable. Thus, the sequential location of a first laugh particle provides hearers information about its referent and its meaning. That people monitor for laughter's referent is evident in phrases like "What's so funny?" or "What are you laughing at?" which call on an interlocutor to account for laughter whose referent is unclear or suspect.

The relationship between laughs and their referents defies consistent labeling, in part because the term *laughable* glosses over an analytically problematic notion. Virtually any utterance or action could draw laughter, under the right (or wrong) circumstances. This fact dooms any theory that attempts to account coherently for why people laugh (see Chapter 1). Although speakers design some turns at talk specifically to provide for recipient laughter (for instance, the punch line of a joke), the distinction between what does or does not count as laughable, or what makes some particular item humorous (a notion overlapping but not synonymous with laughable) remains elusive. I use the term *laughable* retroactively to describe any referent that draws laughter or for which I can reasonably argue that it is designed to draw laughter. Analytical specification of what makes something laughable does not seem a necessary precondition to understanding how people start laughing or laughing together in talk. Rather, I begin with a first laugh and its sequential location, which often provides a relatively clear means for identifying the laughable.

Laughter in coordination with other sounds and actions

When one person is speaking, others may overlap, but such overlaps tend to cluster at turn beginnings and ends, and they tend to get resolved quickly by one or another speaker ceasing to talk (Sacks, Schegloff, and Jefferson, 1974). Extended stretches of overlapping, competing speech may get treated as problematic, and participants have techniques for resolving them (Hopper, 1992, pp. 121–125). As part of this turn-taking system, laughter seems to claim lower priority than speech. Recurrently, laughter-in-progress stops at the onset of competing talk (Jefferson, Sacks, and Schegloff, 1977, p. 3). In this instance, Gene produces an initial burst of laughter, then four particles of laughter. The fourth particle overlaps Patty's resumption of non-laughing speech, and Gene's laughter stops:

([Goldberg:II;1:6] in Jefferson, Sacks, and Schegloff, 1977, p. 3. Gene has been offered a salary of $31,000)

PATTY	Wul knowing <u>you</u> you'd <u>have</u> thirty one en, -thousan and a <u>ni</u>ckel,
GENE	hhh! heh-heh-heh-⌈heh
PATTY	⌊Shit y- I think y'got the original nickel.

As this excerpt indicates, ". . . laughter can be stopped, and recurrently is stopped, when a co-participant signals to the laugher to stop. One such signal is the starting up of talk" (Jefferson, Sacks, and Schegloff, 1977, p. 3). This provides evidence that conversational laughter is controllable and finely coordinated to surrounding activities. It also suggests that speech may take some kind of precedence over laughter in terms of turn-taking distribution – that ongoing laughter will give way to talk but that ongoing talk will not give way to incipient laughter. Given the importance of laughter's sequential placement relative to its referent for the determination of its meaning, this could help reduce ambiguity. The longer laughter competes in overlap with additional talk, the more difficult it may be for participants to recognize which talk (preceding or in-progress) the laughter indexes. Another explanation may lie in the observation that laughs beget laughs – when one appears, often another appears with it. In the instance above, it may be that the resumption of speech cues the laugher that the other speaker will talk rather than laugh, thus diminishing for the moment the likelihood of shared laughter. First speaker may discontinue laughing, with second laugh projectably not forthcoming.

Laughter can serve as a turn-taking cue, or a signal for the next speaker that the current speaker has reached a possible transition point in an utterance. Milford (1977, p. 67) calls this the regulatory function of laughter. O'Donnell-Trujillo and Adams (1983, p. 177) suggest that "[i]n its most robust sense, to laugh is to momentarily lose control of speaking. This momentary ability to formulate speech offers a potential next speaker a place to take a turn." This line of argument assumes that laughing does not share the status of speech as turn-occupying or floor-holding, so that a stream of laughter can be overlapped by speech without being heard as interrupting or usurping a turn. However, it treats laughter as a single unit, whose very presence invites the other speaker to take a turn (presumably, at any point in the laughter; see Schenkein, 1972 on the extra-sequential nature of *heheh*). Yet it is not the presence of laughter per se which invites another speaker to take a turn; rather, transition-relevance places occur within streams of laughter, just as within streams of speech (Jefferson, Sacks, and Schegloff, 1977). Furthermore, the laugher does not necessarily "lose control" or otherwise appear at a turn-taking disadvantage. Rather, laughter appears orderly, and its placement is finely coordinated with surrounding talk and with other laughter.

This may not hold in an environment strongly dominated by playfulness, where attempts to resume speech may lose out. In fact, a person who has been teased or embarrassed may attempt to resume non-laughing speech as a kind of "po-faced" response (Drew, 1987). The laughers, however, may not let the victim off the hook easily. I'll develop this theme further in Chapter 5 on *laughing at* and *laughing with*.

Of course, laughter often appears in the vicinity of other laughter. Although overlapping or adjacent laughs may occur coincidentally and with different laughable referents, the more expectable interpretation is that concurrent laughs are shared, that is, that they align in orientation to the same laughable. Shared laughter is the focus of the next chapter.

Summary

CA provides a set of assumptions and methods that provide a foundation for studying laughter as part of human communication. Insisting on a rigorous, inductive, descriptive science, Sacks and colleagues developed methods that would help them notice order in all, even the smallest, details of talk-in-interaction. Procedures include obtaining recordings of naturally occurring interaction, creating detailed transcripts that attend to all possible features, and searching for order in even the smallest details. Relying primarily on recordings and transcripts, which are shared as much as possible with readers, this empirical science of talk permits checks on claims and accumulations of findings. CA findings connect closely to fundamental concerns in the study of communication. Phenomena identified in CA studies become "tools" by which to investigate new instances of discourse.

Humans laugh in systematic, socially organized ways. Because there is pattern and order to laughter, as there is to all aspects of human conduct, we can study it to learn how people achieve such order. The study of talk-in-interaction utilizes recordings and transcriptions to facilitate describing peoples' methods for organizing talk-in-interaction. Transcription and analysis of laughter reveals patterning in the length and acoustic shape of laugh units and in the placement of laughter in relation to speech, action, or other laughter. The methods and terms introduced in the preceding discussion provide a basis for analyses in subsequent chapters. Specifically, we turn next from characterizing details of laughs in isolation to characterizing the systematic ways people come to share laughter.

3

Laughing together

Laughter is fundamentally social. People do sometimes laugh when alone, but it occurs more commonly in interaction. Furthermore, as research reviewed in Chapter 1 has demonstrated (see p. 26), people are more likely to laugh if others around them are laughing. In many, though not all, social environments, laughs beget laughs, and laughter invites laughter. This shared quality is captured in the lines of a famous poem:

> Laugh, and the world laughs with you;
> Weep, and you weep alone,
> (Ella Wheeler Wilcox, "Solitude,"
> 1888)

Although thoroughly integrated into various other activities, "laughing together" is also an activity in its own right (Jefferson, Sacks, and Schegloff, 1987, p. 158), for which at times people will stop whatever else they are doing. Extended laughings together become memorable, reportable, and storyable events. They offer relationally potent moments which may contribute to group solidarity, developing romance, or hurt feelings. Like other social activities (such as meetings, arguments, and storytellings), laughings together occur, not accidentally or randomly, but through recognizable, systematic means. The focus of this chapter is on how people initiate shared laughter and extend it into lengthier laughings together.

Initiating shared laughter

To understand how laughing together begins, we must examine how speakers create the sequential environments in which it occurs. Because these same environments lead as well to other activities, in the course of examining shared laugh beginnings we will also characterize alternative possibilities.

Shared laughter is not necessarily unison laughter (Jefferson, Sacks, and Schegloff, 1977, p. 2). In this way it differs from other vocal activities such as singing or ritual recitations, for which repetition, rhythm, and other culturally standardized elements enable and oblige speakers to produce roughly the same sounds at roughly the same time. It also differs from talking together. We will hear overlapping speech within the same encounter as competitive, problematic, or chaotic. However, we will hear multiple, overlapping laughs as laughing together, even if their length, acoustic shape, and other features vary considerably. This suggests that once someone is laughing, others can join in at any point without being heard as asynchronous or competing. Nevertheless, the appearance of second laughs following firsts displays precision timing and placement.

Recurrently, conversationalists begin shared laughter not simultaneously but through one speaker beginning to laugh and another joining in rapid succession (Jefferson, n.d., p. 3). A first laugh provides opportunity, perhaps even encouragement, for another to join in laughing. A second laugh shows responsiveness and mutual ratification of a comic or ludic frame. Jefferson (1979, pp. 80–82) characterizes this a sequence of *invitation* and subsequent *acceptance*. Laugh invitations tend to occur either following a turn at talk ("postutterance completion") or while the turn is still in progress ("withinspeech"). In the example below of a post-utterance invitation, Dan completes his utterance then, after a brief gap, provides a first laugh:

(Jefferson, 1979, p. 80)

DAN	I thought that wz pretty outta sight didju
	hear me s̲ay'r you a junkie.
	(0.5)
DAN	hheh₁ heh
DOLLY	⌈hh<u>heh</u>-heh-heh

Dolly's laughter occurs closely following Dan's laugh, but some distance from his utterance, providing evidence that she treats the laugh itself as an invitation rather than the prior talk. The silence following Dan's utterance completion may have been enough to give him reason to suspect that volunteered recipient laughter – that is, offered without invitation – may not be forthcoming. This suggests one reason for first speaker providing a laugh invitation at the completion of a candidate laughable:

> It appears that, in general, the placement of Laugh Units after first completion points in speech or laughter can be geared to defense against a key index of failure of a Laugh Sequence; i.e., the silence which constitutes a lapse in the interaction. (Jefferson, Sacks, and Schegloff, 1977, p. 45)

By laughing while still speaking, current speaker can cue recipient even before the utterance reaches completion that it is laughable. In the following example, within the second syllable of "instihhhks" Mason laughs; precisely following that moment, Jill provides a second laugh:

(SIUC JM)

MASON	You know they have the eh::: huh •hhh most
	beautiful interior decorating (0.4)
	instihhhks⌊ of (0.3)
JILL	⌊fhhhh

At the emergence of a first laugh particle by current speaker, even though the utterance may not be complete, second speaker can recognize the laughability of the emerging utterance and respond with a second laugh. Placing laugh particles within an utterance can make it possible for shared laughter to be in progress by the time the current turn ends. In this way, participants provide for prompt, timely shared laughter.

First speaker can produce an *equivocal* laugh particle that could be laughter or a breath, part of a word, or an exclamation. If the recipient laughs, the first speaker can then add more laughing sounds, so that the first sound can be heard retroactively to have been a laugh invitation (Jefferson, 1979, p. 89). Here, Jeff produces an audible inbreath. Then he and Vana both produce outbreath laughs. With the occurrence of these, his preceding inbreath can be heard to have been laughter:

(Jefferson, 1979, p. 89)

JEFF	en Ramsbach's in there lyin there with a smoke
	(.)
JEFF	•hh hh⌊ ehhhh
VANA	⌊aaahhh!

Equivocal laugh particles can be retroactively framed according to subsequent events as having been laughter (if the recipient produces a next laugh) or as something else (if the recipient does not laugh). This equivocality allows offerer to put forward the possibility of shared laughter with a minimized risk of failure, that is, of extending an invitation that gets refused.

In contrast to the invited laugh shown above, voluntary laughs – those produced without prior explicit laugh invitation – do occur routinely. They themselves may get treated as first laugh inviting a second. In the following excerpt, C laughs during A's story at a moment which isn't noticeably laughable, or even transition relevant. Evidence that this laugh is asynchronous and misplaced may be seen in the fact that A does not acknowledge it in any way, but continues with her story.

(SIUC CB1 94)

> A   for- for her ↑birthday. And just knowing
>   Ro:b mean, I could just see him telling them
>   that (.) this gift that came in you know this
>   package₁ that came from Penney's.=
> C   ⌈hhhahahahaha

Jefferson (1979) describes three possible courses of response following an invitation to laugh. Recipients may *accept* the invitation by laughing, *remain silent*, or *decline* the invitation, usually by speaking "seriously" on some topic. A standard format for beginning shared laughter includes laughable plus laugh invitation by current speaker and second laugh by someone else. Here, Ellen produces an utterance including standard comic devices of a contrastive pair ("big things/little things") and ironic reversal. She laughs, then Bill produces a second laugh, accepting her invitation and joining in shared laughter:

(Jefferson, 1979, p. 81)

> ELLEN   He s'd <u>well</u> he said <u>I</u> <u>am</u> <u>cheap</u> he said,
>   •hh about the <u>big</u> things. he says but not
>   the <u>liddle</u> things, hhhHA HA HA₁ HA HA
> BILL   ⌈heh heh heh

Another recipient option is *silence*. The invitation offerer can
orient to silence as a sign of trouble, indicating that recipient does
not understand the laughable, does not treat the laughter as inviting
more laughter, etc. However, recipient silence does not disengage the
relevance of more laughter; in fact, an offerer may treat silence as an
opportunity to pursue the possibility of shared laughter (Jefferson,
1979, p. 83). In the next example, Cara first invites laughter via a
within-speech laugh particle (line 418). In the gap that follows Rick
could respond but remains silent:

(UTCL D8a. Cara says she has a female houseguest coming to stay
with her. Rick asks if the guest will share Cara's bed. A lengthy
interchange follows, in which Rick indicates that if any of his (male)
friends came into town he would share Rick's bed and Rick "would-
n't even think about it.")

415	CARA	Wull (.) ↑That's pro'ly what (me an ___) -I
416		mean I (just don't know her very well?)
417	RICK	₍Uh huh
418	CARA	⌐(But it's) rully no(h) big d<u>ea</u>l.
419		(0.8)

Cara pursues laughter by producing another laughable displaying
both within-speech laugh particles and post-utterance laughter. The
within-speech laugh particle brings acceptance from Rick, indicated
by his laughter onset immediately following her particle and prior
to her utterance completion:

418	CARA	(But it's) rully no(h) big d<u>ea</u>l.
419		(0.8)
420	CARA	She c'n sleep in my bed if
421		she (h)unts to₍ (h) huh ↑huh ↑huh?₎
422	RICK	⌐<u>hhh</u> ehh eh uh⌐=

To disengage the relevance of the laugh invitation, Jefferson argues, recipient must actively decline it (see also Lippert, 1998). One
way to do this is by resuming non-laughing speech (Jefferson, 1979,
pp. 83–84). In the following, Ida is relating a conversation she had
with her son in which she offers to come for him if he has "hurt himself or something." Within the word "self" she embeds two laugh
particles. Immediately following these particles, Jenny overlaps the

utterance to provide speech, specifically a first pair part question containing no laughs:

(Rah:II:10)

```
10      IDA      =cz – (ih) se t a̲h:'ll pop round if yiv
10a–12           h̲eu:rtchise(h)e(h)₎ lf (or someth' •hh)
11      JENNY                         ⌈What ti:me d 'e ri⌉ng.
```

By talking, Jenny discontinues the relevance of Ida's prior laugh invitation. Ida ratifies the move to non-laughing talk by discontinuing her laugh particles.

In the following example, Stacy invites laughter within and following the word "morning." There is no response. Stacy pursues the laugh invitation by another particle within the word "wondering"; again, no recipient laughter is provided. Following utterance completion, Mom asks a first pair part question which implicates topic shift. Stacy laughs again, gets no second laugh, then moves on to non-laughing speech.

(SIUC S1)

```
STACY    And he was really mad cuz I didn't come home
         until like one-thirty in the mornin(hh)g nhn
         huh huh and he was calling my room
         w(h)ondering where I was.
MOM      Well so what else is new?
STACY    uh huh huh huh huuh
         (2.2)
STACY    I think we should like mark this on the
         calendar=
MOM      =How long=
STACY    =Over a week=
```

Speaking in the next turn does not necessarily constitute declining an invitation to laugh. Two features appear relevant to how participants work this out: the seriousness/playfulness of the speech, and the possible presence of smiling. Jefferson's examples show recipients disattending humorous or playful aspects of laugh-invitation turns and taking up their serious import. However, a recipient may choose to sustain the humor or playfulness yet not actually laugh in response (Haakana, 1999, p. 59).

(West, 1984: Dyad 10: 675–686, in Haakana, 1999, p. 60)

```
01   PATIENT   Yestidy ah uz- (.) tellin' (0.2) Mary, ah giss
02             it wu:z,
03             (.)
04   PHYS      Um-hm.
05             (.)
06   PAT       •h Docktuh Wilbur nevuh ha:s hurt me:.
07             (0.4) hunh-hunh-hunh[ hunh-hunh! Ye-hunh-hunh]
08   PHYS                          [Now yuh can tell'er       ]=
09   PAT       =[-hungh-hunh. •h!]
10   PHYS       [that's   not   true!]
11   PAT       •hh!=
12   PHYS      =Climb dow:n, an' put back yer- (0.2) blou:se
13             on
```

In this example, the patient makes a joking implication that the
physician has "hurt" her. In overlap with the laughter, the physician
produces non-laughing speech. Although this fits the pattern of a
declined laugh invitation, it can be seen that the physician's talk
sustains the playfulness of the patient's comment. He "goes along"
with the joke without actually laughing.[1]

Lavin and Maynard (1998) posit a third option between accepting and declining: responding with a smile voice or pseudo-laugh,
which can display recognition that mirthful response is relevant, yet
withhold an unambiguous form of such a response, which might
constitute an unduly affiliative display. They provide audio transcript examples of interviewers responding this way when interacting under normative constraints against laughing along with interviewees. For example, the interviewee responds to a question,
then shows uncertainty about the answer, followed by laughter. The
interviewer does not laugh along but does respond with a smile
voice.

([PC08:2344:032:SS:606–621] in Lavin and Maynard, 1998, 16)

```
01       FI     What is the NAME of the other religious group
02              that contacted you?
         ((lines deleted))
09       FR     I believe it's the Congregational Church.
10              (0.6)
```

11	FI	O::k:::↑ay
12		(2.0 typing during silence)
13→	FR	I have no idea rilly I (been) heh heh heh
14→	FI	Ok↑a:::↑y ((smile voice))
15		(1.8)
16	FI	N:::OW I have some questions about your
17		neighborhood . . . . . .

Although in most cases the second laugh arrives immediately, it may be delayed by a *side sequence* (Jefferson, 1972) devoted to some interactional issue relevant to the laugh invitation. The side sequence business being accomplished, the second speaker can then provide recipient laughter, its relevance having been postponed but not terminated. Two examples of this occur in succession in one conversation. In each case, Rick produces a candidate laughable plus laughter. In the first one, Cara initiates a side sequence repetition of Rick's laughable with questioning intonation. Rick provides the second part to this side sequence by reasserting his laughable, without laughter. The side sequence completed, Cara provides the second laugh that was invited three turns earlier. While Cara may have initiated this side sequence to repair some kind of hearing or understanding difficulty, she may also produce it as a means of sharing Rick's laughable with Leigh Anne, who is co-present with her but cannot hear Rick's voice directly from the phone.

(UTCL D8a. Side sequence utterances are marked with brackets on left of speaker identification.)

516	RICK	But ↑I'm going to go-=
517	RICK	=↑I'm'nna go r- ra:n now.⌐ °hh-hh-hh°
518→	CARA	⌐>Y'gonna go<ran?
519→	RICK	'm 'nna go ⌐ra:⌐n.
520	CARA	⌐nh⌐ha ↑ha ha ha.=

A few turns later, Rick provides a "wrong" version of a playfully incorrect verb form. Cara suspends laughter to initiate a repair sequence amending this laughable. Rick reasserts the repaired version of it, accepting and completing the side sequence repair. At this Cara provides the delayed but still relevant recipient laughter:

529	RICK	An then I'm gonna go::un to a movie. °hh hh°
530		(.)
531→	CARA	Gunna gone to a movie?
532→	RICK	Gonna go:ne to a ⌈mov(h)ie.
533	CARA	⌊eh ↑hih hih hn ↑hn hn •hhh

In the instance above, Cara is able to withhold her laughter while co-constructing the side sequence, then resume full, mirthful laughter. The fact that a recipient can hear a laugh invitation, take part in a side sequence, and *then* produce responsive laughter provides further evidence that laughter is not simply an uncontrollable, instinctive reaction to a stimulus. It is organized, systematic, and finely coordinated with features of surrounding talk.

Of course, many laughs occur in interaction without getting a second. Are these all examples of second speaker declining opportunities to laugh? This raises methodological issues concerning the interpretation of conduct that does not occur. In principle, any person can laugh at any time, so the absence of laughter does not automatically prove meaningful for participants or analysis. Therefore, it is analytically important to identify when laughter is *noticeably* absent; that is, when some action has provided for its relevance. Shared laughter can constitute a show of participant alignment in orientation towards the laughable referent. Sometimes, however, such alignment does not appear to be the recurrent pattern. When a speaker is telling about troubles (Jefferson, 1984) and laughs, routinely the listener does not laugh but offers a "serious" response to the topic of the preceding utterance. In this example, S treats her utterance "I've stopped crying" as laughable, whereas the recipient G does not orient to the prior laughter as an invitation to laugh:

([Frankel:TC:1:4:SO] in Jefferson, 1984, p. 346)

G	You don't want to go through all the ha:ssle?
S	•hhhh I don't know Geri,
	(.)
S	I've I've stopped crying uhheh-heh-heh-heh-heh,
G	Wuh were you cry::ing?

The first utterance does not do the work of a first turn laughable inviting laughter. Rather, laughing while troubles-telling displays a posture of "troubles-resistance" on the part of the speaker; that she/he is managing, in control, etc. (Jefferson, 1984). It is the recipient's job to take the troubles seriously, to respond without laughter; in other words, to show "troubles-receptiveness." For recipient to laugh would not display affiliation but rather refusal to take the trouble seriously, more akin to laughing at the first speaker than with (see Chapter 5).[2] Haakana (1999) shows examples in medical interviews of patients laughing while complaining of symptoms, resisting doctors' advice, or talking about delicate matters. Commonly doctors do not laugh along. Here, Haakana argues, patient's laughter is not inviting the doctor into shared laughter but rather demonstrating an orientation to the laughable. The doctors tend to provide non-laughing, serious uptake of patients' talk. A related example appears below, from a health appraisal interview between a patient and a physician's assistant.

(SDCL:Kaiser/lines 168–186, in Beach and Dixson, 2000, p. 8)

INT	=home as well. •hh And then the demands at home are from your husband on one side and your children on the other. •hh And basically the only time that I hear that you have for your<u>self</u> is once a month on a Thursday night when you go to church.<
PAT	°Right°.
PAT	₁Hhhh uh huh₁
INT	⌈That doesn't⌉ sound like very <u>much</u>.
PAT	£It's not much. £ ₁•hhhh heh hhh₁
INT	⌈° O k a y °⌉. <u>Tell</u> me about depression=Has that been an issue for you.

The patient's laughter marks her own orientation to her problematic situation. It does not work to invite shared laughter, nor does the interviewer treat it as such. Rather, the interviewer sustains serious treatment of the topic.

Everyday interaction shows plenty of evidence of speakers formulating, describing, narrating, accounting, and more in ways that demonstrate orientation to coming off as something like "normal." This preoccupation (Sacks 1984 describes the doing of "being ordinary" as a speaker's "job" in conversation) appears to drive the laughter produced while one is recounting troubles or complaining. Similarly, people recounting paranormal experiences (Avery and Antaki, 1997) recurrently laugh either following mention of the strange phenomenon or following the description.

(Informant 1, Paranormal story, in Avery and Antaki, 1997, p. 11)

> INF   I got up out of bed (.)
> and went to where the toilet was
> and the door was open
> and there was nobody there
> and there was absolutely ↑no:body in the house
> (.)
> and I was (.)
> so: (.) petrified
> ((laughs))
> >I got dressed straight away<
> and shot out of the house
> as if Old Nick had got me (.)

The authors characterize such laughter as a "normalizing device" – marking the teller's distance from the told – particularly important in telling of a paranormal experience for which the teller's sanity might be questioned.

If first laughable is directed at co-participant (by teasing or making that person appear unfavorably) then first laugh by laughable-producer can be understood as doing something other than inviting shared laughter. Rather, it works to disaffiliate. In the following, Lynn assesses Beth's statement about the weather. Within each of the key assessing terms, "pro↓fou(hh)nd ↓sta(h)tetemen(hh)," she embeds laugh particles.

(SAA: BL, in Armstrong, 1992, p. 138)

> 16   B   You know (0.2) it c'n ↑either stay h<u>o</u>t or it
> 17   could stay co:↓ld but-
> 18   (1.8)
> 19   L   Well now that's a pro↓f<u>ou</u>(hh)nd ↓st<u>a</u>(h)temen(hh)
> 20   B   We(hh)ll (.) I mean like >if it gets< h<u>o</u>:t?

```
21              ↓it's gonna stay hot and never cool do:wn?=>but
22              if it's< (.) you know if it's ↑coo:l it's always
23              cool.=D'ju notice?
```

For the butt then to join in laughing might be understood as an attempt to transform the situation back to a more affiliative one. However, the point is that the first laugh does not seek out shared laughter,
but rather displays antagonism, however mild, towards the recipient. This is discussed in Chapter 5 on *laughing at* and *laughing with*.

Likewise, volunteered first laughs (produced by other, treating
previous speaker's talk as laughable) may show disaffiliation and
not invite shared laughter. In the following example, Donna informs
Jay that she is recording their telephone conversation and asks for
his consent. Instead, he laughs, displaying resistance:

(UTCL A16)

```
JAY        (I guess-) Good athletes they=they play in pain
           though don't they.
           (0.6)
DONNA      I guess so:=I'm making another tape okay?
           (0.3)
JAY        hu huh •hh hh=Why:
```

Jay's laughter comes in a second pair part position (following her
request for consent) as part of a turn showing dispreferred structure (pause, delayed or absent rejection component, expanded talk
on topic). The laughter works disaffiliatively. Similarly, Haakana
(1999, p. 253) provides examples of doctors laughing at what patients say, when patients have provided no explicit laughter or other
marking of their own humorous orientation to their talk. In such
cases, the doctor's laughter may be showing refusal to take seriously
the patients' complaints. The idiom "laughing it off" captures this
sense of laughing to show refusal to take seriously something by
previous speaker. Sacks (1992, pp. 12–20) shows how friends and
family members use "laughing it off" as a response to suicide threats
which involves refusal to take them seriously.

Keeping in mind that laughter carries multiple meanings and can
do many things, it is not surprising that not all laughs invite shared
laughter. If laughter works to display a perspective towards the
laughable that cannot or should not be shared by co-participants,

then it does not operate as a first laugh invitation. For recipients to laugh along might constitute a breach needing remedy; not shared laughter but misalignment. This then brings us back to a smaller subset of instances in which first laugh invites but does not receive second laugh. In such cases Jefferson's explication remains relevant. Recipients commonly will decline the laugh invitation and discontinue its relevance by pursuing non-laughing, serious talk on topic.

In some interactional environments there are normative constraints on participants' options to invite shared laughter or to accept such an invitation. Anyone who has ever tried unsuccessfully to suppress laughter at some inopportune moment (e.g., an orchestral concert, a funeral, a meeting) has experienced this sense of constraint. Television entertainment-show hosts will laugh along with their guests; however, journalistic news interviewers generally will not. Whether affiliative or hostile, laughter can easily be heard as violating the neutrality expected of (at least some) participants in institutional interactions. Information-gathering interviewers may specifically be instructed not to laugh along with their interviewees, as in instances analyzed by Lavin and Maynard (1998). Normative constraints against laughter also appear to influence medical care providers who tend to laugh less than patients and tend not to laugh along when patients laugh first (Haakana, 1999).

Although the vast majority of instances of shared laughter begin with one person laughing, there are cases in which two or more speakers begin laughing simultaneously. If one of the laughers is laughable-producer, then that person's laugh probably stands as an invitation to laugh. Recipient's simultaneous laugh would likely constitute a volunteered laugh that arrives while other speaker is proffering an invitation. In the following example, Cara produces a laughable (line 178). Immediately following utterance completion, she laughs (179); at the same time, Rick laughs while beginning a next turn of speech (180):

(UTCL D8a)

169	RICK	£Well£ do you kn<u>ow</u> 'er?
170		(0.3)
171	RICK	°h°=
172	CARA	=Do I kn<u>ow</u> 'er?
173	RICK	Yeah.
174	CARA	I mean I kn<u>ow</u> 'er,

175	RICK	Eoh hh!
176		(.2)
177	RICK	O̲h you <u>know</u> h<u>e</u>r eh!
178	CARA	But I don't kn<u>o</u>w 'er.=
179	CARA	=₍h<u>uh</u> hh •₍hhh₎
180	RICK	₍(h)you doh huh huh- ₍ uh.₎

Cara's laughable (line 178) is one in a series of turns containing rapid-fire word-play, possibly tinged with sexual innuendo. It is the fourth consecutive turn to end with "know her"; that repetition may facilitate simultaneous onset of laughter by providing both a highly projectable laughable and completion point of the laughable.

Visual features of shared laugh beginnings

Much of what we know about the sequential organization of shared laughter comes from analyzing audio recordings, often of people talking on the telephone who cannot see each other. This is not surprising, for early CA research drew from audio recordings of talk. Beginning in the 1970s, conversation analysts took advantage of the growing availability of inexpensive video equipment to begin studying visual aspects of interaction (see Goodwin, 1979, 1984; Heath, 1984; Schegloff, 1984; and many more recent studies). The extent to which studies based only on audiotape are unduly limited, or that telephone talk offers only limited generalizability to face to face, is a matter of debate and empirical investigation. A host of CA research bears out Schegloff's (1979) claim that "the talk people do on the telephone is not significantly different from that they do face to face" (p. 43) in terms of sequential organization. How people organize laughter seems consistent across data drawn from both face-to-face and telephone interactions; that is, whether or not participants have access to each other through visual channels. (The fact that those who are visually impaired can readily join in shared laughter provides further evidence.) However, laughing is an embodied experience, and we perceive it through both sight and sound. Smiling, shaking of head or torso, crinkling of eyes, and other possible indicators of laugh onset may figure prominently in how people begin laughing together when they can both see and hear each other. In this section, some consideration is given to visual features of shared laugh beginnings. This also expands phenomena of investigation to include smiling as well as laughing.

Many CA studies of the past twenty years have examined visual aspects of interaction. Specific to laughter, Wrobbel (1991) analyzed behaviors of stand-up comedians leading up to delivery of punch lines. He found comedians establishing a baseline of behavior (casual delivery, gazing straight ahead) then forecasting the punch lines with changes in eye gaze, body position, tempo, etc. From analysis of videotaped patient–physician interactions, Haakana (1999, p. 62) provides evidence for smiles constituting a middle option between laughing and not laughing. A smile indicates some acknowledgment of pleasure, amusement, friendliness, or alignment, yet does not implicate respondent in shared perspective as fully as would laughter. Whether these work to forestall further pursuit of shared laughter or not remains an issue for empirical investigation.

The instance presented below unfolds in a manner parallel to others examined already: first laugh invitation, declination, pursuit, and shared laughter. However, examination of the video record reveals ways in which eye gaze and smiling contribute to the unfolding of this stretch of talk. Specifically, the recipient of a first laugh invitation smiles as a placeholder until completion point of the laughable utterance and subsequent invitation, at which time recipient provides minimal laughter. Smiling shows willingness to engage humorously or playfully. Recipient displaying willingness to engage humorously, before actually laughing, gives laughable-producer a warrant to help set up the moment of shared laughter by forecasting it through laugh pre-invitation. In short, the move into shared laughter seems more subtle and gradual than previously understood.

This bit of talk takes place during a two-party, face to face interaction in which partners Jill and Mason are in their kitchen. Talk on a previous topic has ceased and there is a six-second pause. Jill lifts up what looks like a small (perhaps three-inches tall) white bust. Their talk in reference to and touched off by the bust unfolds as follows:

(SIUC JM)

1		(6.0)
2	MASON	Beethoven?
3	JILL	Beethoven. (0.4) kh •hh ((click-noise))

4	JILL	You no(tice) Bart and Linna have one of these=
5		I think it's Mozart?
6	MASON	Oh ⌜yeah?⌝
7→	JILL	⌞like ⌟ on thei(h)r <u>hh</u> eh
8	MASON	Do they?
9→	JILL	£Yea(h)h on their pia(h)no⌜£ (0.8) •ehhh
10→	MASON	⌞hhh
11	JILL	I ↑think they've had that since like (0.7) <u>uh:</u>
12		their kids were y<u>ou</u>ng (.) you know and I was
13		goin' over there with Bobbie which was probably
14		(0.8) °hhohh man° I donno- cause ↑Tracy plays
15		piano. She did.=
16	MASON	=Ri:ght
17		(2.0)

Of particular interest are lines 7–10. In line 7 Jill laughs within the word "thei(h)r" and for two particles following it. Mason does not laugh along but declines the invitation by talking on topic, with the first pair part question "Do they?" which shows uptake on her unfolding news announcement. At line 9 Jill replies affirmatively to his question and adds talk done with a smile voice and with laugh particles embedded within the words "Yea(h)h" and "pia(h)no." Following the latter, Mason produces one particle of laughter. After an inbreath laugh particle, Jill resumes non-laughing talk on topic. In brief then, these lines include the following:

Laugh invitation/declination

| 7 | JILL | like on thei(h)r <u>hh</u> eh |
| 8 | MASON | Do they? |

Pursuit of recipient laughter through reinvitation/acceptance

| 9 | JILL | £Yea(h)h on their pia(h)no£ ⌜(0.8) •ehhh |
| 10 | MASON | ⌞hhh |

Jill laughs initially at what would seem an odd location for inviting recipient laughter. The words "like on thei(h)r" do not complete a turn pragmatically or syntactically, and they do not provide any clear laughable for which Mason might claim recognition.

Furthermore, Jefferson (1979) has shown that when recipient remains silent following first laugh, inviter will pursue laughter, but
that recipient talking constitutes active declining of the laugh invitation. Here, however, Mason talks, yet Jill pursues laughter. Examination of visual features provides more nuanced understanding of these
matters.

Entering the field of play. When Jill first picks up the object
Mason notices her doing this and walks towards her. The slight hint
of amusement in his voice as he says "Beethoven?" suggests playful
orientation. Jill turns Beethoven out towards Mason and pushes the
bust slightly forward while making a clicking sound. The effect is a
playful "presentation" of the bust to him. They now are co-focused
in attention on the bust and have both displayed playful framing of
it. Jill asks a question that makes use of the bust as a topic:

4	JILL	You no(tice) Bart and Linna have one of these=

It would be relevant now for Mason to answer, but before he can
do so, she rushes past the completion point of this first pair part
to produce another turn constructional unit, "I think it's Mozart."
She ends this second part with upward, "try-marked" intonation
that indicates uncertainty and helps link it to the preceding first pair
part question to which his answer now is relevant. As a "news re-
ceipt" (Maynard, 1997, p. 107) Mason's reply shows a retrospective
orientation, acknowledging what she said as news yet discouraging
further topical development of it.

4	JILL	You no(tice) Bart and Linna have one of these=
5		I think it's Mozart?
6	MASON	Oh yeah?

Mason is looking down. On her word "Mozart" he looks up in one
sweeping head–eye movement to the bust then to her eyes. After
uttering "Oh" he looks back down again. Following procedures
developed by Goodwin (1979), in the transcript below Mason's eye
gaze is indicated in smaller font on the line below the talk with
which it co-occurs. A word (such as "bust") shows he is gazing at
that object, and a solid line shows continuation of the gaze. Commas
indicate eye gaze moving away, and periods indicate movement of

eye gaze towards the named referent. No indication means he is looking down or away:

```
5       JILL        I think it's Mozart?
        MASON                    ⌐bust__.⌐Jill⌐
6       MASON       ⌐Oh yeah?
        MASON       ⌐Jill,
```

They now have demonstrated willingness to engage playfully regarding the bust, and they have talked about it.

Laugh pre-invitation. In overlap with his reply, just as his eye gaze drops from her, she continues talking, and her talk contains laughter within the word "their" and for two following particles:

```
6       MASON       Oh ⌐yeah?⌐
7       JILL            ⌐like  ⌐ on thei(h)r eh uhh
```

The talk within which her laughs occur can be characterized as a delayed completion (Lerner, 1989). It is added onto a previous, hearably complete, turn constructional unit, and it is added on in overlap, disattending and sequentially deleting Mason's talk. However, this delayed completion itself is not yet complete: the possessive pronoun "their" needs a referent (perhaps it's more appropriately termed "delayed continuation"). Reconstructed, her turn-in-progress reads like this:

> JILL   You no(tice) Bart and Linna have one of these=
>   I think it's Mozart? like on thei(h)r eh uhh

Placement of the laughter suggests that it anticipates rather than follows the laughable. Because Mason does not yet have the referent available to him, this laugh does not seem to invite shared laughter. It does help prepare an environment for shared laughter to follow; thus it seems to be doing the work of pre-invitation. Accompanying the laugh particles following the word "their" Jill makes a sudden head movement forward. Immediately following this movement and her laughter, Mason looks at her face and smiles. In the transcript below, Jill's head movement is shown above her laughter; Mason's smiling is indicated by the smiley-face emoticon "☺" and a solid line:

5   JILL   I think it's Mozart?

         MASON   ᒋbust__.[Jillᒋ

6   MASON   Oh ₁yeah?₁

         JILL   [   ]   ₁moves forward

7   JILL   [[like ᒋon thei(h)r <u>h</u>ᒋh eh

         MASON   ᒋJill,   ᒋJill

         MASON   ᒋ☺___ =

It seems that Jill's laugh particles and head movement work to bring Mason's gaze to her (see Goodwin, 1979 for analysis of how speakers draw recipient gaze) and his face up, revealing to her a smile.

Display of willingness to laugh. In speaking (line 8), Mason does not laugh and his non-laughing talk would seem to discontinue the relevancy of laughter. However, he continues smiling and gazing at her (shown in small font below spoken words):

6   MASON   Oh ₁yeah?₁

         JILL   [   ]   ₁moves forward

7   JILL   ᒋlike ᒋon thei(h)r <u>h</u>ᒋh eh

         MASON   ᒋJill,   ᒋJill

         MASON   ᒋ☺___ =

8   MASON   Do they?

         MASON   ᒋJill___,ᒋ

         MASON   ᒋ☺___ =

Mason's next turn, like his preceding one, orients back to the announcement, two turns earlier, that Bart and Linna have "one of these." In contrast to "Oh yeah?" however, "Do they?" works as a "newsmark" (Maynard, 1997, p. 108) to encourage topical development. His continued talk is not redirecting topic but rather inviting her to develop this one more. Mason is providing space for her to develop the laughable, while showing through his continued gaze and smile, his willingness to appreciate it.

Laughable + laugh invitation, acceptance: shared laughter. Jill's next turn both responds to his first pair part with the single word "yeah" and continues and completes her turn in progress. She produces this utterance with a "smile voice" and particles of laughter embedded within the first and fourth words.

9   JILL   £Yea(h)h on their pia(h)no£

Following the word "piano," Mason provides one exhaled, voiceless laugh particle. Then Jill laughs on an inbreath, and their brief
moment of shared laughter ends. However, Mason continues smiling
at her.

```
 9   JILL     £Yea(h)h on their pia(h)no£ ⌈(0.8) •ehhh
10   MASON                                ⌊hhh
     MASON     ⌈☺_____
```

Jill resumes speaking, without laughter, about Bart and Linna.
Mason looks down at a piece of string he is holding. The playful interchange seems to have ended (although, interestingly, he maintains
his smile for several more moments).

```
11   JILL     I ↑think they've had that since like (0.7) uh:
     MASON     ⌈☺_____
12   JILL     their kids were young (.) you know and I was
     MASON     ⌈☺_____⌋
13   JILL     goin' over there with Bobbie which was probably
```

Movement into and out of shared laughter, as well as into and
out of playful frames, appears much more interactive and nuanced
than previously reported.

Having visual access to each other allows participants to prepare
the ground for the emergence of a moment of shared laughter. In
the instance just examined, two speakers establish willingness to engage playfully regarding a referent (the bust of Beethoven). In their
subsequent talk, Jill's first laugh does not mark a laughable moment
but projects that it is forthcoming. Showing sensitivity to this, the
recipient (Mason) does not yet laugh but smiles and maintains gaze
to show readiness to laugh. Upon completion of the laughable utterance she proffers a second laugh invitation, to which he provides
brief second laughter.

Evidence from this instance suggests that a smile constitutes some
mid-point between laugh along and declining to laugh. Similar to
Lavin and Maynard's claim that a brief laugh may accomplish something midway between fully sharing laughter and declining to laugh,
we may understand smiling as an alternative to laughing or not
laughing. In this instance, smiling precedes laughing and displays
willingness to go there.

Extending shared laughter

Shared laughs cease at systematic completion points unless participants specifically act to keep them going. A decline in volume, cessation of sound, or shift to inbreath may all signal a transition relevance place at which someone may resume speech or other activities.
Yet shared laughter does get extended, and people accomplish this
in ways that are stable and describable. Three ways to extend shared
laughter are discussed below: extension of laughter without more
laughables; re-invoking a first laughable; and offering a next in a
series of laughables.

Extension of laughter

Participants may renew laughter beyond the transition relevance
places at which a stream of laughter might cease. Extending laughter can occur on its own or in conjunction with extending reference
to the laughable or providing new laughables (shown below). A
next laugh particle following a possible laugh completion may initiate renewal of laughter and provides a basis for keeping *shared*
laughter going. In contrast, participants may pre-empt the possibility of renewing laughter by talking before a completion point in the
laughter occurs. In the following example, Kate spies "puppy poop"
on the bottom of Brandon's shoe. Her laughter floods out through
her utterance reporting this observation:

(UTCL D6. They are sitting on the ground in a city park, and he
now is checking his clothing to see what smells like "puppy poop")

	KATE	Check the bottom of your sho<u>oe</u>:s.
	BRAND	Do I look n<u>o</u>rmal?
		(1.1)
→	KATE	Looks like it's uh(h)↑on th(h) ↑'ott(h)om
→		huh hih (.) shoo(h)oo
		(0.2)

Following an inbreath and brief pause, she produces a six-part laugh
unit. A pause follows, then another inbreath laugh particle, and
another brief pause:

	KATE	Looks like it's uh(h)↑on th(h) ↑'ott(h)om
		huh hih (.) shoo(h)oo
		(0.2)

→   KATE   •↑ehh (.) huh <u>huh</u> huh <u>huh</u> huh <u>huh</u>
                (0.6)
→   KATE   •ehh (.)

The pauses and inbreaths signal possible completion of laughter as
well as a turn-transition place. Brandon is silent, however, producing
neither laughter nor speech at this point. Kate renews laughing with
a lengthy stream of laughter (fourteen syllables before the inbreath):

                (0.6)
      KATE   •ehh (.) huh ↑huh ↑huh ↑huh (.) huh huh huh huh
                hah hah huh huh huh huh (.)
                •↑ehh ↑huh=

Renewal of laughter allows for the possibility of laughter extending
beyond the natural limits of a single breath or partial breath. It also
provides a way to "grade" laughables. Prolonged laughter marks
a laughable as unusually funny or noteworthy. The occurrence of
prolonged laughter itself becomes an event that may be talked about,
questioned, celebrated, or laughed about. Kate's lengthy laughter
here displays her as "cracking up" over the odoriferous discovery
on Brandon's shoe. Combined with his silence, her extended laughter
may point to an interactionally problematic moment in which one
participant finds something exceptionally funny while the other does
not find it at all laughable.

    As this example shows, one way to extend laughter is simply to
renew laughing following possible completion points. Extension of a
solo laugh may invite extended shared laughter. Yet laughter cannot
continue indefinitely by itself, and this process of extending laugh
units in reference to a single laughable may have natural limitations
(Jefferson, Sacks, and Schegloff, 1977, p. 18), as the laughter gets
farther in sequential time from its referent.

Extension of a single laughable

Participants may re-invoke a previously successful laughable, via
repetition or reference to it, providing a sequential basis for shared
laughter to continue. When laughter occurs, hearers will search for
its referent in the immediately preceding/ongoing activity or talk.
The further it strays from its referent, the more problematic may
be its association with that item. In addition, it seems that shared

laughter cannot continue indefinitely without more stimulus materials. Re-introducing the preceding laughable provides a solution to both these problems. It brings the laughable forward sequentially, and provides a basis for extending shared laughter. Reintroduction of a preceding laughable gets accomplished through repeating all or part of it, or making some reference to it.

The following instance shows extension of a single laughable occurring in conjunction with the first technique described above, extension of shared laugh units themselves. The participants are reading aloud and appreciating inscriptions written on Carlin's birthday card. Talk moves momentarily away from the card. Jan redirects attention to it by a question. The others remain silent while she reads a remark she attributes to Peter (a priest at their church who is not present at the time of the recording).

(UTCL J2)

JAN	Yu what does ↑he mean.
	(1.2)
JAN	Peter says haven't been that hot before,

Hearers treat this utterance as laughable. Carlin produces one particle of laughter, and one male and one female speaker laugh together.

JAN	Peter says haven't been that hot before,
CARLIN	uhh!
(MALE)	ehh heh ⌈heh ⌈heh heh heh heh
(FEM)	⌊heh ⌊heh heh (heh heh)

After this laughing, Carlin initiates repair by objecting to the accuracy of the reading. This shifts focus from the "meaning" of what Peter wrote to Jan's reading of it. Carlin follows this with a stream of five particles of laughter (it is difficult to tell whether subsequent, quiet laugh particles are from her or someone else). A brief pause follows. One (female speaker's) inbreath laugh displays termination of laughter, while one (male) speaker produces a particle that may be starting up a new stream of laughter.

JAN	Peter says haven't been that hot before,
CARLIN	uhh!
(MALE)	ehh heh ⌈heh heh heh heh heh
(FEM)	⌊heh ⌊heh heh (heh heh)
CARLIN	⌊I don't think 'e ↑SAID THA:T!=

```
CARLIN          =eh huh huh ↑hah hah
                ((brief noise–perhaps chair creaking))=
(F)             =•eₜhh
(M)              ⌈hu-
```

Carlin's repair initiator prompts Jan to self-correct the reading. She now does so, in partial unison with Carlin. Speech floods into raucous laughter.

```
(F)             =•eₜhh
(M)              ⌈hₜu-
JAN              ⌈Oh haven'tₜ↑seen thatₗ
CARLIN                         ⌈↑seen thatᴵ=
(J or C)        =HₜA! uh HAₜH        ⌈   •eh-uh
(J or C)         ⌈HAH!   ⌈HAT!   ⌈BEFORE.=
```

In treating this moment as laughable, wildly laughable, the participants are most likely orienting to a sexual meaning of "hot." Previous inscriptions have teasingly assessed Carlin ("sweet and kind," "Yankee") making relevant treating this comment too as assessing her. The subsequent repair from "been" to "seen" and "hot" to "hat" changes referent from Carlin to a hat and to a safer, more innocuous reading (this instance nicely illustrates the Freudian theory of laughter resulting from release of tension prompted by sexual matters; see Chapter 1).

At least three speakers produce a first round of shared laughs. At the appearance of Carlin's inbreath particle while the others have momentarily stopped, a possible winding down in the shared laughter seems evident:

```
JAN         Oh haven't ₗ↑seen thatₗ
CARLIN                  ⌈↑seen thatᴵ=
(J or C)    =HₜA! uh HAₜH        •eh-uh
(J or C)     ⌈HAH!   ⌈HAT!   ⌈BEFORE.=
CARLIN      =AH HAH! ₗHAH! ₗHAH!ₗ
(?)                    ⌈↑huh! ⌈huh! ᴵ huhₜ! (.) hah hah huhₗ
ED                              ⌈eh heh! heh! heh!ᴵ=
            heh hah hah
J           •euhhh
```

Participants simultaneously renew laughter and reintroduce the laughable. Ed repeats part of the preceding laughable. Overlapping this, Carlin renews laughter with a high-pitched shriek:

```
J                    ⌈•euhhh
ED          =⌊(      )  ⌊Ha:t before.⌋
CARLIN                 ⌊↑u:::::::::h⌋
```

Ed renews his laughter. They approach a next possible completion point, as Ed ends his laugh stream and Carlin produces three consecutive inbreaths.

```
ED          =hoh-hoh ↑hoh- ⌈hoh hoh- hoh.        ⌋
CARLIN                     ⌊•euhh- •euhh •ehhh⌋
```

Again participants continue the shared laughter. Carlin renews laughing with a Step Up through increase in volume and a shift from closed- to open-mouthed laughs. As her stream winds down, Wilson and another (female) participant add laughs:

```
CARLIN      u↑AA:H HUH- HAH HUH-HEUH
            heuh⌈-↑huh
WILSON           ⌊ehh hih-hih-⌈hih-   heh   h⌈euh=
(FEM)                         ⌊eeh-euhh ↑hh?⌋
```

Overlapping Wilson's laugh, Jan makes a lexical reference displaying appreciation of the laughable ("I love it"). Renewed laughter and lexical appreciation markers follow:

```
CARLIN      u↑AA:H HUH- HAH HUH-HEUH
            heuh⌈-↑huh
WILSON           ⌊ehh hih-hih-⌈hih-   heh   h⌈euh=
(FEM)                         ⌊eeh-euhh ↑hh?⌋
WILSON      =he:⌈ ::h
JAN             ⌊↑I ⌈↑l::ove it,
TARA                ⌊°•ehh°
(FEM)       uhh-⌈ huh-   huh⌋
TARA            ⌊↑(Mym)y-  ⌋ ⌈ huh-huh⌋
CARLIN                        ⌊a:h huh- ⌋ ↑hah-huh
            °euh-huh •ehhh°
```

The multiple laugh units comprising this extended shared laughter serve to celebrate the mis-reading of the birthday card. Through a combination of partial repeats, lexical references, and renewed laughter, participants keep the original laughable centered as the object of group appreciation. Individual speakers do not laugh continuously, but collectively, the participants provide for the relevance of, and produce, continuing shared laughter orienting to a single laughable.

Extension of multiple laughables

Participants can create additional laughables that cohere thematically or structurally with a preceding one. By extending the laughable topic or device, speakers provide opportunities for laughing together. Vicki and Shawn have been talking about a mutual friend. Matthew produces a first pair part seeking clarification in which he characterizes this friend as "the guy who comes out and treats you." Following a brief pause, Matthew affirms the answer to his own question. Vicki too affirms and laughs following this reference and Shawn joins in laughing:

(CD:II:40. TS by G. Jefferson)

MATTHEW	The guy ('oo) comes out'n tr<u>eat</u>s yuh?
	(0.2)
MATTHEW	Y<u>e:</u>⌈h.
VICKI	⌊Yhh ⌈e(h)eh
SHAWN	⌊heh heh ⌈h<u>e</u>h h<u>e</u>h heh- ↑<u>e</u>h⌉
VICKI	⌊<u>i</u>hh h<u>u</u>h-huh- hu⌋:h

Three inbreath laugh particles appear in succession, the first and third by Matthew, and the second by Vicki. These constitute possible completion points for shared laughter:

VICKI	Yhh ⌈e(h)eh
SHAWN	⌊heh heh ⌈h<u>e</u>h h<u>e</u>h heh- ↑<u>e</u>h⌉
VICKI	⌊<u>i</u>hh h<u>u</u>h- huh- hu⌋ :h
MATTHEW	⌈•ih=
VICKI	=•h ⌈h C<u>o</u>me ⌈o u t⌋ a g <u>a i</u> :n ⌉
MATTHEW	⌊•<u>hehh</u> ⌊<u>huh</u> hu⌋h hu ⌋

Now Vicki produces a next laughable, done as a performed calling to the friend to "come out (to their city) again." Matthew provides renewed laughter. His first laugh particle arrives after Vicki has

uttered only one word of her turn and its placement here may suggest that it orients to the prior laughable rather than to the one Vicki
is now producing:

```
VICKI       =•h ⌈h  C̲o̲me ⌈o  u  t⌉ a g a i̲ :n⌉
MATTHEW         ⌈•hehh    ⌈huh hu̲⌊⌉ h hu    ⌉⌉
```

Nina produces another laughable, an upgraded (with "please") version of Vicki's preceding request to the friend. Vicki provides more
laughter.

```
VICKI       =•h ⌈h  C̲o̲me ⌈o  u  t⌉ a g a i̲: n      ⌉
MATTHEW         ⌈•hehh    ⌈huh hu̲⌊⌉h hu         ⌉⌉
NINA                      ⌈C̲o̲:me out ⌊ple̲ ⌋a̲:se.
VICKI                                     ⌈hhe̲:h̲ heh
            he h-eh
```

Shawn produces a next laughable which, like the prior ones, is done
as if spoken to the friend, asking the friend to come out because
Shawn is "runnin' a little short" (of money). He places a laugh
particle within the word "out." Following this Vicki renews her
laughter. Shawn completes his utterance and appends three more
laugh particles to it. Matthew also adds laughter:

```
VICKI       hhe̲:h̲ heh he ⌈h-eh
SHAWN                     ⌈Whe̲n you comin' o̲u(h)t
            aga⌈in um r̲unnin a  lih sh⌈o̲:rt.ih ⌈h he̲h⌉ h e h ⌉
VICKI          ⌈mm-hm-hm-h u̲ h -h̲ u h⌉      ⌈     ⌉       ⌉=
MATTHEW                                     ⌈ih hn̲⌉ ya ha⌉
```

Shawn produces another laughable extension. This time, however,
he adds no laughter. Vicki produces non-laughing talk at a completion point in his turn, and the shared laugh extension seems to be
ending:

```
SHAWN       =•hh I fi̲ll like hev'n a good ti:me.⌈ (I yiss)
VICKI                                           ⌈W'l'e̲e̲
            estuh e̲arn a lotta mo̲ney before'e c'd °come°
```

Matthew produces a laughable, in overlap with Vicki's bid to resume
non-laughing talk. His new laughable gets followed by recipient

laughs from Shawn and Vicki, achieving further extension of shared laughter:

VICKI	W'l'ee estuh
	⌜earn a lotta money before'e c'd⌝
MATTHEW	⌜I j's lost my j o : b.⌝
VICKI	°co ⌜me°
SHAWN	⌜uh ha⌜h huh hu⌝
VICKI	⌜unh huh hu ⌝nh

There is then a pause and resumption of non-laughing, "serious" talk.

In summary, an earlier reference to the friend brings shared laughter. Participants then generate a series of laughables on this same topic. Not all the laughables get shared laughter, but several do, and the cumulative effect creates an extended cluster of shared laughs. This is the third means by which speakers extend conversational shared laughter: extending multiple laughables that are thematically or sequentially tied to the prior.

Discussion

Commonly laughter is shared; commonly shared laughter starts through an invitation–acceptance sequence. Speakers invite laughter by placing laugh particles within their turn at talk or following it. Placement of a first laugh invitation facilitates shared laughter. If done within-speech, the invitation provides an early recognition point that allows the recipient to be laughing by the time the utterance reaches completion. This reduces the chance of a noticeable gap, such gaps possibly indicating failure of a laugh sequence. If done post-utterance, the laugh invitation fills the first space at which a gap might occur, again preventing possible failure. It also allows recipient an opportunity to laugh along with current speaker at utterance completion, if recipient can at that point recognize utterance's laughability without invitation. A first laugh may be equivocal, enabling speaker to retroactively display it as not-laughter if it does not generate recipient laughter. Recipients may treat a first laugh as an invitation to laugh unless the laugh is produced within a specific sequential context, such as troubles-telling, where it can be seen to be doing other kinds of work than inviting recipient participation. This "default" value, generally to treat first laughs as invitations, provides for shared laughter. These features – placement and timing, possible equivocality, and status as invitation – allow speakers to extend laugh invitations while minimizing the possibility of, and consequences of, failure to generate acceptance. They make it easy for recipients to join in laughing in a timely manner; if recipients decline, they give offerer opportunities to mitigate sequential import of the rejection.

Responses to laugh invitations, too, seem organized to facilitate shared laughter. A second laugh, provided in a timely manner, constitutes acceptance of the laugh invitation. Silence in place of the second laugh typically brings pursuit by first speaker, thus providing another opportunity for shared laughter. Only continuation of talk without laughter by second speaker constitutes declination of the laugh invitation. When this occurs, the sequential focus then turns on the ongoing talk rather than on the declined invitation. Again, these features serve to provide for shared laughter and reduce the consequences of invitations that do not get accepted. They provide evidence that conversationalists orient to the social desirability of laughing together and to the difficulties that can arise when recipient laughter is sought but not provided.

The label *volunteered* applies to first laughs by someone other than current speaker, for which there is no first laugh by current speaker and for which the laughable does not seem expressly to invite laughter. Yet there may also be instances in which a laughable, rather than first laugh, serves as a laugh invitation. Jefferson (1974, p. 6) notes that both laughables and laughter, singly or in combination, may invite laughter. Jefferson, Sacks, and Schegloff (1977, p. 30) propose that a sequence of laughable plus recipient laughter may constitute an *adjacency pair*, suggesting that a laughable by itself makes laughter relevant from next speaker. The question then arises as to whether a first laugh from someone other than current speaker should be labeled as volunteered or invited. This is an issue of analyst's vocabulary, which is intended to provide insight into participant orientations. Because laughables are so diverse it remains difficult to present a consistent case for their status as specifically inviting laughter or not, except for specialized interactional moments, such as the punch line of a joke.

Once in progress, shared laughter naturally reaches termination points rather quickly. Conversationalists must actively renew shared laughter. Three methods for doing so include extending laugh units themselves, reinvoking a laughable, or adding a next laughable to provoke more shared laughter. Each method allows for displays of different orientations to the laughable referent(s) and to self and other(s). After first shared laughter occurs, speakers can simply renew laughing through a next laugh invitation and acceptance sequence. The possibility of renewed laughter must be negotiated along with possibilities for resumption of talk. Yet this technique seems limited, as conversationalists do not appear to extend shared laughter for very long without introducing new objects to serve as its sequential referents. A second method involves recycling a prior laughable by repeating all or part of it or making lexical reference to it. This makes the laughable sequentially current, allowing for renewed or extending appreciation of it via more shared laughter. Third, speakers can provide for extending shared laughter by producing next laughables showing topical or structural relevance to preceding ones. A single speaker may produce a succession of laughables and may also join in the shared laughter; or various speakers may contribute laughables in succession. In such cases, turn transitions become points of negotiation about who will take next turn, whether that turn will be laughable, or whether that turn will contain, or consist solely of, laughter. The sequential roles of laughable-producer and laugher(s) shift rapidly or even blur in such episodes.

Instances of multi-party extension of multiple laughables seem to fit Bormann's (1981) use of the term "dramatizes." Originally developed from coding schemes in Bales' (1950) research on group interactions, "dramatizes" describes members of a group jointly developing fantasy themes through their talk. Sometimes, Bormann reports, dramatizing communication

would chain out through the group. The tempo of the conversation would pick up. People would grow excited, interrupt one another, blush, laugh, forget their self-consciousness. The tone of the meeting, often quiet and tense immediately prior to the dramatizing, would become lively, animated, and boisterous, the chaining process, involving both verbal and nonverbal communication, indicating participation in the drama. (Bormann, 1981, p. 16)

Shared laughs regularly occur in the environment of dramatizing talk. For these activities a series of shared laughs is both an outcome and a signal. One manifestation of fantasy theme chaining through interactants is shared laughs (though not necessarily so). Shared laughs, in turn, display such co-participation in the dramatizing activity. In this regard, the absence of laughter from one or more speakers might mark non-participation in the dramatizing activity.

Among the three techniques for extending shared laughter, is any kind of contextual ordering evident? When, if ever, do speakers orient more to extending laughter, a single laughable, or a series of laughables? The first two maintain sequential focus on one laughable as the referent for extended appreciative displays. Prolonged appreciation may show orientation to that laughable as particularly "funny." People routinely evaluate laughable materials on the basis of how successfully those materials generate laughter and other appreciations. Thus we need standard, knowable ways to display to others and ourselves that we find something more than usually laughable. For the individual, physiological manifestations of hysterical laughter may show this (such as trembling, doubling over, tears in eyes, etc.). Interactively, people can show exceptional mirth through extended laughter and references to the laughable.

More broadly, people may show that they find something meaningful by maintaining, past its completion, its relevance as present focus of talk or activity. Filmgoers will leave a theater reliving lines, moments, and emotions through their talk. Audiences orient to a particularly good live performance by extending applause longer than usual, bringing performers out for bows, curtain calls, and encores. An exciting moment in a televized sporting event gets shown repeatedly, analyzed, and talked about, often interspersed with shots of cheering crowds and elated teammates. Similarly, hearers treat a great laughable as such by extending displayed appreciation of it. Such an extended display comes about through these first two multispeaker devices, expansion of laugh units and reinvoking laughables via repeat or lexical reference.

Extension via production of additional laughables displays a different emphasis. A cluster of laughables helps generate a cluster of shared laughs. Participants' focus moves sequentially to the next laughable. Cumulatively the laughables display participants aligning in their view of the imagined comic situation. Shared laughter extension displays appreciation of a progressive series of laughables rather than protracted appreciation of a single one.

Conversationalists display the importance of shared laughter by providing places for it in talk and providing means to keep it going once it has begun. Shared laughter can display co-orientation or alignment of laughers, remedy interactional offenses, and provide a sequential basis for displays of conversational intimacy. Extended shared laughter marks an episode of celebration in talk. To those taking part, the laughter may feel overwhelming and unstoppable. As this research demonstrates, however, the progression from beginning to laugh together to extending shared laughter is methodical and sequentially organized.

Variations in how people accomplish initiating shared laughter allow for other activities to be accomplished in and through it. One such variation concerns who issues the invitation and who responds. Participants rarely begin laughing together at the same time, and in principle any co-present party may laugh first. Do people orient to constraints on who should or may not initiate shared laughter? Whether current speaker or someone else laughs first, whether there are third or more other parties co-present, and the sorts of sequential activities in which participants are engaged all bear on how shared laugh sequences get started. These issues provide the focus for the next chapter.

4

Who laughs first

Because shared laughs begin recurrently through a sequence in which one person's laughter invites others to join, the issue of "who laughs first" becomes an important one.[1] From a conversation analytic perspective this question gets framed sequentially. Identity is treated in terms of "who" holds the floor and is current speaker; who is some co-present other; who offers an invitation to laugh; who is the recipient; who is teasing; who is the victim of a tease; who is telling about troubles; etc. These sorts of "who"s shape (and get constituted through) the organization of talk in specifiable ways. Participants orient to them, and they are demonstrably relevant to the analysis of shared laughter initiation.[2]

"Current speaker" designates the party (usually an individual, but possibly a group, as in the case of audience laughter) who occupies a turn at talk and has some degree of rights and/or obligations to produce speech and/or action. "Other" designates participant(s) not holding the turn at talk. These terms reflect the premise, put forth by Sacks, Schegloff, and Jefferson (1974), that turns are a scarce resource, available only to one party at a time. Although this is not essential, people in all sorts of interactions organize their participation in this way. The sequential roles "current speaker" and "other" come up for grabs at each transition relevance place (TRP) (Sacks, Schegloff, and Jefferson, 1974). In order to suspend these rules so that one may occupy a longer turn at talk, speakers may, for example, bid for rights to tell a story before actually starting the telling (Sacks, 1974). This does not necessarily prevent others from taking a turn or stopping the story telling, but it strengthens the relevance of current speaker continuing beyond a single "turn construction unit" (Sacks, Schegloff, and Jefferson, 1974) until story completion.

Sacks, Schegloff, and Jefferson (1974) outline three basic devices by which next speaker is selected. In the first, current speaker selects a specific next speaker. This can be done by using an address term, or by an utterance such as a question, offer, or invitation (these are called first pair parts of adjacency pair sequences) which strongly implicates an answer by a particular other person. In the second device, current speaker completes turn and any next speaker may self-select. Third, if no other speaker self-selects, current speaker may start speaking again. In such case, the talk may retrospectively be heard as continuing current speaker's extended turn at talk. However, it is not always clear to participants – or, thereby, to analysts – who holds the floor. The terms "current speaker" and "other" capture participant orientations, but they should not be taken to mean that participants always know or clearly display which role they or other(s) occupy at any particular moment.

With that caveat, we turn to examining how participants organize the beginning of shared laughter with reference to the sequential roles of "current speaker" and "other." Jefferson (1979) suggests this distinction by terming a first laugh from current speaker a laugh "invitation," while first laugh from other she terms "volunteered" laughter. One can readily perceive interactional consequences of whether the current speaker or some other laughs first. To laugh at one's own remark or action suggests an awareness of its laughability, perhaps even intention to be laughable. For other to laugh first may display that current speaker did not produce talk or action as intendedly laughable. I will return to these possibilities in the discussion in Chapter 5 about *laughing at* and *laughing with*.

As a starting point, then, we can observe that either the current speaker or someone else may provide the first laugh in a shared laughter sequence. In this example (discussed in Chapter 3) Mason laughs during the word "instincts," a humorously critical assessment of the tastes of some people they know. Responsive to his laugh particle, Jill provides a second laugh.

(SIUC JM 99)

MASON	You know they have the eh::: huh •hhh most beautiful interior decorating (0.4) instihhhks⌈ of (0.3)
JILL	⌊fhhhh

In the following example Carlin is reading aloud greetings and comments that people have written on her birthday card. At Ed's prompting, she reads what he wrote, which apparently includes a description of her as a "Yankee." Following this she begins laughing.

(UTCL J02)

ED	And ↑I said wh<u>a</u>t.
	(3.0)
CARLIN	Sweet and k<u>i</u>:nd.
	(0.7)
(JAN)	°(iy)<u>A</u>w::hh°
	(1.2)
CARLIN	<u>Y</u>ankee ehh-h<u>e</u>h h<u>a</u>h ↑hah hah₍ °huh-huh°
JAN	₍eh h<u>i</u>h h<u>i</u>h h<u>i</u>h hih

By laughing first, Carlin displays to the others that what she read is laughable, and she invites them to share laughter with her. Jan orients to this invitation by joining in laughing.

In the next example, Wilson gives a humorous answer to Jan's question. At the completion of Wilson's utterance Terri provides an initial laugh syllable, and at least two other participants join in shared laughter:

(UTCL J2)

JAN	what were y<u>ou</u> doin sixteen years ago.
	(2.0)
WILSON	Havin fu:n,
TERRI	a<u>a</u>hh!₍ huh
JAN	₍e₍hh!
ED	₍heh hehheh heh huh.

Terri laughs following Wilson's utterance completion. Jan and Ed laugh immediately following her first particle, displaying onset-sensitivity to her laugh and thereby constituting this as an invitation–acceptance laugh sequence. The invitation, however, is not from Wilson, who produced the laughable.

The first two examples show shared laughter beginning with first laugh from the current speaker and the latter shows shared laughter begun by someone else. What factors influence this matter of

Table 4.1 *Initiation of shared laughter in conversation: by speaker(current or other) and by number of parties (two or multi)*

Type of interaction	First laugh by current speaker	First laugh by other	Simultaneous first laugh
Multi-party	33	112	4
Two-party	49	11	7

participant choice? What local consequences derive from who laughs first? How does initiating shared laughter, or withholding first laugh, contribute to participant understandings of meaning, relationship, circumstance, or self? It turns out that "number of parties" in the interaction is relevant to who laughs first. As I was first transcribing and analyzing instances of shared laughter, I noticed an interesting trend. Most of the time, when two people were talking (usually on the telephone), the current speaker would laugh first. Most of the time, when three or more people were talking (usually face to face), someone other than current speaker would provide first laugh. The table above combines data from two different collections, both showing the same pattern.

It seems that in two-party talk, current speaker generally (87% of the cases) laughs first. In multi-party interactions, the current speaker rarely laughs first (17% of the cases). What is going on in particular situations which would contribute to this tendency?

That the number of parties affects the organization of who laughs first is not surprising, for prior research has shown it to be fundamentally important to the organization of interaction. The number of parties potentially competing for the floor affects the turn-taking system (Sacks, Schegloff, and Jefferson, 1974, pp. 712–714). In two-party interactions the person currently not speaking will have an opportunity at next turn without having to compete with other participants. With three or more parties the possibility arises that any particular current non-speaker may not get the next turn, and techniques for next-speaker selection become particularly salient. In multi-party settings a bias operates in favor of shorter turns: each possible transition relevance place in the ongoing turn presents possibilities for speaker change, so current speaker may be constrained to keep turns short and minimize points of possible competition for the floor. With four or more speakers, the possibility emerges for sub-conversations of at least two parties each. In short, the number of parties in interaction strongly influences the availability of, and workings of, various turn-taking options.

The numbers reported above suggest a general trend across a number of instances. However, the focus of our analysis is on identifying participant orientation within particular instances to rules of sequential organization. What evidence in the talk might there be to explain this distribution? If general rules of social organization are at work, how do we account for the exceptional cases? Let's turn now to consider some cases of shared laughter beginnings to see what sense might be made of the preponderance of "current speaker laughs first" in two-party interactions and "other(s) laugh(s) first" in multi-party interactions.

Multi-party shared laughter: other laughs first

In multi-party interaction, greater flexibility exists in the ways that shared laughter may begin. Current speaker may produce laughable, some other may begin laughing, and other(s) may join in. Thus shared laughter can begin without the participation of current speaker or one or more other persons in the encounter. We can understand this as an additional degree of freedom in the interactional possibilities for starting shared laughter in multi-party interaction. In this example, Stanley produces a laughable utterance. Sondra initiates laughter overlapping the end of it, Jerry joins in, then Stanley participates as a third:

(UTCL A30a. Stanley has returned after being away from the phone for a couple of minutes while Sondra and Jerry continued to talk.)

8	STAN	°Y'all missed° that ↑hi̱ke
9		in cu:nver ₍sation.
10	SONDRA	⌈Mhh! hmm₍ hmm h₎ eh!
11	JERRY	⌈eh hi̱h! ⌉
12	STAN	u̱h hi̱h •hhh

In the following example, Roz "sets up" Tammy by providing a first pair part question about Tammy's son, Jabbar. Recipient laughter from Roz and May follows Tammy's laughable response:

(UTCL A30b. Tammy is mother to Jabbar, a pre-school aged boy. Roz and May may be Tammy's relatives.)

```
4     ROZ       Jabbar been playin' wit ⌈h his whi:stle.
5     TAMMY                              ⌊°•e:::::::::h:o::h.°
6     TAMMY     ↑GIR:L.
7               (0.3)
8     TAMMY     Blowin spit e:v'ryweah,=
9     ROZ       =h⌈ hnh ⌈ hnh?⌈ hu̲a̲h ha⌈ h    ⌈ °•ehhh°
10    MAY          ⌊°↑hih ⌊↑hih ⌊hih.°     ⌊Didn' ⌊I te(ll) you
11              all⌈ ah t↑o̲'d you . . .
12    ROZ         ⌊°ehh-huh-hih°
```

Current speaker holds perhaps the best position to laugh first. If that person is producing a laughable, he/she can earliest anticipate its emergent laughability. Current speaker can embed laugh particles within the emergent utterance, where recipient overlap is less likely, or append laugh particles upon utterance completion prior to or in overlap with recipient responses. By virtue of already holding the floor, current speaker should, by rules of turn-taking, have first option on self-selecting to continue, with speech or laughter (Sacks, Schegloff, and Jefferson, 1974, p. 704). Given these considerations, why would a current speaker *not* laugh first? Across many cases of multi-party shared laughter, why do current speakers routinely not laugh first? Put another way, why do current speakers in multi-party interactions routinely opt for producing laughable *only* rather than laughable *plus* first laughter?

Conversationalists regularly face the task of displaying or figuring out laughter's referent. Because laughs are locally responsive, generally some current talk or action serves as the laughable. When someone speaks and then laughs, the laughter likely indexes the speech (although that speech itself may in turn refer to or reinvoke some other speech or action). Among the variety of conversational laughables, some appear specifically designed to make volunteered recipient laughter relevant, with current speaker having ownership of the laughable. In the first of the two preceding examples, Stanley suggests that his presence provides a "hike in conversation." In the

second, Tammy produces a humorous description of her child, trying
to play a whistle but "blowing spit everywhere." In each, exaggeration and idiosyncratic word choice emphasize laughability; each is
produced such that the author can take credit for it. For such items,
laughter can serve as recognition of their success, perhaps even as a
form of praise. Jokes, for example, represent a specific category of
these laughables; the barometer of a successful joke is its ability to
draw laughter. Although tellers may not claim original authorship,
they do claim credit for successful delivery of the joke. Given this
feature of ownership, there may be a participant bias against current speaker providing the first laugh. Laughing first at one's own
designedly laughable materials may be heard as engaging in self-
praise, akin to a public speaker applauding herself for making an
effective oratorical point. Standup comedians rarely start laughter at
their own jokes; they will, however, laugh after the audience members have begun laughing.[3] Then, the laughable-producer's laugh is
sequentially tied to recipient laughter rather than to the now more
distant laughable, and thus does not constitute self-praise. When
comment is made about someone laughing at his own joke, it is
not the laughter itself but the laughing first that seems to constitute
a "violation." A similar bias against self-praise operates for other
conversational features, such as compliments (Pomerantz, 1978,
p. 81) and may operate for laughter. In one-to-many communicative
settings and multi-party conversations, current speakers routinely
produce laughables only and others (audience members) initiate
laughter.

   In this group conversation about an upcoming Superbowl, Lana
presents her method for deciding which team she will support.
Wilson overlaps the end of it with an exaggerated "oh" response.
He uses information Lana provided in her prior talk to construct a
laughable answer (lines 5, 8–10) for her decision-making procedure:
she will have to root for the 49ers, since Cincinnati players are old
(and, therefore, not handsome). A brief gap follows, then Ed and
Carlin begin shared laughter:

(UTCL J2)

1	LANA	(ll) ↑I̲('ll) tell you wha̲t Wilson I̲'ll take a
2		good lo̲o̲k at the players on bo̲:th teams.
3		And the team that has the m↑o̲:st handsome ones

4		that's⌊ the one I vote fo-r.

4   that's⌊ the one I vote fo-r.
5   WILSON   ⌈O↑o:::h. Theh' 'scuse m↑e then we̲ll I
6   guess-
7   (1.1)
8   (?)   °⌊(h-m hm hm)°
9   WILSON   ⌈I guess the Fo̲rty NI̲ners.
10   Cause all the Cincinnati have too many
11   o̲l' ones.
12   ED   hu⌊-h heh he-h heh
13   CARLIN   ⌈°heh heh⌊ h-eh°
14   WILSON   ⌈eh huh huh huh heh heh hah hah

Ed then Carlin begin the shared laughter. Wilson joins in, but only as third laugher, not initiator. Interestingly, Lana, with whom this interchange began, does not laugh. This may have something to do with her role in this interchange as the "straight man." Wilson asked her whom she would root for, she answered, and he made a laughable based on her answer. Her answer, though, contains elements that seem potentially humorous and set her up as an object for tease or continued talk: she watches football not for the sport, but for the handsome men. Wilson's next laughable develops the idea of the teams having handsome players but does not pick up on Lana as viewer. Thus her answer is used as a springboard for his laughable, not as a laughable in itself. In this way, she is made the straight man for this sequence, and neither she nor Wilson provide first laugh. The presence of multiple others who can independently initiate shared laughter makes this configuration possible.

Another kind of collaboration occurs in the next instance. Here a participant who possesses prior knowledge about the laughable cues others when to laugh by initiating shared laughter. Shawn and Vicki (one couple) have just completed a jointly produced story about Shawn driving the wrong way down a street. Michael offers a possible story beginning by turning to Nancy (his partner) and asking a question that orients to some experience that he and Nancy have shared. Nancy's strong response displays that she remembers and finds the referent laughable. Michael provides a second laugh to her initiation. (Interestingly, Vicki too laughs, even though she does not at this point have information to appreciate the referent's laughability in the same way the others do.)

(CD: II: 74. TS by G. Jefferson)

MICH   'Member the wah- <u>guy</u> we sa:w?
            (0.2)
NANCY   ehh↑ (h)<u>Oh</u>(h)o he₍e Y(h)   ₍a(h) ah <u>ha</u> <u>ha</u>₎
MICH   ⌈huh huh ⌈   ⌉=
VICKI   ⌈ihh h<u>i</u>h heh heh₎
NANCY   =₍<u>ha</u> ↑ha
VICKI   =⌈heh •ehh

This cues the other couple from the outset that the story to come is laughable and that shared laughter will be relevant. In telling the story, Michael describes a car going down the street sideways, with its "fuckin' frame" cracked. Nancy laughs during his utterance, adding "It was so funny." But the others offer no laughter here, and Nancy's laughs drop out as Michael resumes telling:

MICH   But (0.7) <u>fi</u>rst'f all wee see this <u>ca</u>r goin
            down the street ↑side↓ways. Its
            f₍ u ck in'₎   fra₍me is ₎ c:<u>ra</u>:cked.₎
NANCY   ⌈°↑hn ↑hn°⌉   ⌈•hihh⌉ Ih wuz ⌉h ih huh
            so₍ (h) o f <u>un</u> n y.₎
MICH   ⌈Inst<u>ea</u>d'v a <u>ca</u>r go⌉ in' down th'
            str<u>ee</u>t downa street like=

Michael produces another laughable utterance; during its final word "this" he changes a hand movement from pointing straight ahead and moving forward to turning sideways while continuing to move forward. There is a brief gap after the utterance completion, at a point when the hand gesture change is recognizable. Nancy renews her laughter and Vicki simultaneously begins laughing:

MICH   Inst<u>ea</u>d'v a <u>ca</u>r go in' down th'
            str<u>e</u> ₍et downa street li₎ ke=
NANCY   ⌈•h e h h •<u>i</u> h h h⌉
MICH   =₍this goin-like t₍<u>hi</u>s.₎
NANCY   ⌈ihh: i h h : :   ⌈<u>hi</u>h⌉
            (.)
VICKI   ₍ihhh:: ₍huh–<u>hu</u>₎
NANCY   ⌈uh ↑<u>ha</u> ⌈ <u>ha</u> ha- ⌉ ah↑ ha ↓ha •ihhhh

Again Nancy provides first laugh to Michael's laughable talk. The presence of two speakers who are familiar with laughable materials (such as a story or joke) permits this division of labor. Michael, the storyteller, does not initiate shared laughter. Nancy collaborates, not as co-teller but as respondent to events narrated, via her appreciation markers ("it was so funny") and her initiation of shared laughter. By these acts she cues the other two participants to the relevance of laughter at key points in the story. Furthermore, she relieves Michael of either (1) having to initiate laughter at his own laughables, or (2) risking failure to elicit recipient laughter at relevant points.[4]

Participant bias against self-praise may operate for laughables hearably designed to draw laughter. Some laughables, however, seem unwitting, such as a speech error, faux pas, or talk which displays naivety. In these cases current speaker may not initially orient to the laughability of his/her utterance or action, but some co-present other(s) may. The next example shows the workings of shared laughter with a naive current speaker. Wilson, with assisting comments from Ed, has been describing activities associated with betting on football games. Ed asks Wilson a question about specific details of the gambling operation (lines 1–2). Ed could have posed his question to display that he does not know anything about such activities, e.g., "How is the operation set up?" Instead, by asking whether the numbers run one way or another he displays that he knows there are such numbers on a board, and thus that he has some knowledge of betting pools. Overlapping the end of his first pair part question, before Wilson can answer it, Jan asks about the legality of such activities:

(UTCL J2)

ED	Are the numbers from one to ten that way or one to ten that ⌐way.⌐
JAN	└ Is ┘ that legal?

Her question carries with it a candidate answer (Pomerantz, 1988) that betting pools might be legal. She might have posed it in a way that implicitly asserted clearer prior knowledge on her part, e.g., "Isn't that illegal?" She could have added her own first laughter, displaying this question as joking acknowledgment of the impropriety

of the activities of which her co-participants display knowledge. By
not laughing first, Jan orients to her question as a "serious" question and not as a laughable. A long gap follows, at which either Ed
or Wilson might provide a relevant second pair part. Ed begins a
drawn-out, comic "well"; the combination of a gap and the dys-
fluency marker "well" can display a dispreferred second pair part.
Overlapping the "well" Wilson bursts into laughter, and Ed adds a
particle of laughter:

JAN	Is that legal?
	(1.1)
ED	W::⌈ell ↑heh⌉
WILSON	⌈eh! heh!⌋ heh heh hueh hah huah huah.

By the comic response and shared laughter, Ed and Wilson orient to
her question as laughable, perhaps naive. Several turns later, Wilson
answers Jan's question, and both men further display knowledge of
the topic:

WILSON	•hh ri::ght. No it's not really legal.
	(1.5)
WILSON	See it's causeuh- see its gamblin see?
ED	eh They won't putchyou in jail fer it.

In this instance, current speaker does not laugh first but produces
a question as sequentially serious. Two other participants initiate
shared laughter at this seemingly innocent question; they are the
ones who make it, retroactively, into a laughable.

In the example just shown, shared laughter displays like-
mindedness among two of three speakers. Such alignment need not
occur by accident; in the next example, current speaker specifically
provides for two recipients to align and share laughter at his laughables. Several turns prior to the moment in question, Stanley tells
his side (Pomerantz, 1980) of having had difficulty reaching Jerry.
Such a device can make relevant from its recipient an account of
what he has been doing. Jerry initially remains silent; Stanley provides another utterance, this time referencing Jerry by name. Jerry
provides an account for why he's been hard to reach, doing so in a
"character" voice: lower register than usual, and more modulated
delivery.

(UTCL A30a)

STAN	Tr↑ied to git 'n <u>tou</u>ch wi'chyou
	(earlier) man but its (da:mn) you jis' so
	hard tuh (1.3)
STAN	I- <u>I</u> jis' don' know 'bout chyou
	Je⌊rry.
JERRY	⌈Well you kn<u>o</u>w it's the little w<u>o</u>man.
	She keeps me goin.

Stanley treats this account seriously by displaying sympathy with
it. Sondra produces a tease by asserting that Jerry has no woman,
"little" or otherwise. Stanley joins in the tease, and Sondra expands
on it, suggesting that the reason Jerry is hard to find is not a woman
but slothfulness:

(Some TS lines omitted)

STAN	°eh::::: I heard d<u>a</u>t shi:t.°
	((lines omitted))
SONDRA	'E ain' got no woman eh h<u>u</u>h (uhh)
	((lines omitted))
STAN	<u>He</u> don' have no sweet°⌊(heart)°⌋ t'take care of
SONDRA	⌈°righ'.°⌉
STAN	do'e=He jes'be.
	(0.7)
STAN	Perpetr<u>a</u>t'n,
	(0.8)
SONDRA	Exacly 'e sl<u>ee</u>ps all day lo:ng.

Jerry responds with a serious, "po-faced" (Drew, 1987) response to
the tease that he has no sweetheart:

SONDRA	Exacly 'e sl<u>ee</u>ps all da⌊y lo::ng.
JERRY	⌈You say I got
	w<u>o</u>menuh.
	(0.2)
JERRY	(feel uh rouh) I have a woman.
	(1.1)

Stanley builds on Sondra's previous turn teasing Jerry about sleeping
all day. He addresses it to Jerry (he is the "you" and the "man" in
it) and shifts the focus of talk from Jerry to Sondra: the issue now

is not whether Jerry sleeps all day, but that Sondra said Jerry sleeps all day. Following a gap at which Jerry could respond but does not, Stanley continues the shift with a next utterance which again references "she":

STAN	She sai'ya sleep all day ma:n?
	(1.6)
STAN	She could be.

Stanley starts, but does not complete, a turn suggesting some possibility: "could be." He announces that he will not say whatever it is he was going to say. One possibility is that Stanley is implying that Sondra knows Jerry's sleep habits because of an intimate (sexual) relationship, thus teasing both Jerry and Sondra. They both laugh:

STAN	She sai'ya sleep all day ma:n?
	(1.6)
STAN	She could be.
	(1.5)
STAN	No woh won' say that,
SONDRA	uh⌊-h! hheh heh heh heh⌋-heh •hh
JERRY	⌈eh teh (.)heh-h↑ih heh-h↑ih⌋

Stanley has converted a two-on-one tease with Sondra of Jerry into a one-on-two tease of Jerry and Sondra. He has also shifted the focus again: not just that Sondra has intimate knowledge of Jerry, but that Stanley will not say what he was going to say.

This laughable retrieves two items from previous talk: Jerry claiming he has a woman and Sondra claiming that, instead, he just sleeps all day. It uses these items to suggest another alternative, teasing both Jerry and Sondra: that Jerry's "woman" is in fact Sondra, and that's why she knows his sleeping habits. By starting an utterance, cutting it off, and not completing it, Stanley invites the hearers to solve the puzzle by filling in the missing pieces. The partial utterance plants the hint of sexual innuendo without actually doing so explicitly, then disavows the entire procedure. Through the disavowal, it calls attention to its author, Stanley.

Teasing sets up a laughable *at* rather than a laughing *with* relationship between teaser and victim (see Chapter 5). With multiple participants, two or more may do the teasing and two or more may get teased. In either case, the two or more have the opportunity to laugh together, displaying like-mindedness towards the referent. The current speaker Stanley, by constructing talk in which he alone teases two recipients, creates a sequential environment in which the two may laugh together as victims. That they do so ratifies their shared orientation towards the laughable. Having no other co-teaser with whom to share laughter at the expense of Jerry and Sondra, Stanley does not laugh.

In addition, since the solution to the puzzle created by his incomplete utterances may be a tease with sexual innuendo, the others can display their success at having figured it out by laughing. Sacks (1974) suggests that dirty jokes serve as understanding tests; recipients can display their savvy by laughing at the punch line. In a similar way, this implied sexual tease might invite the others to display through laughter that they get Stanley's drift.

The foregoing considerations do not necessarily replace or preempt the notion of participant bias against current speaker laughing first in multi-party interactions. Rather, they are presented to suggest that the organization of who laughs first may orient to multiple sequential and relational features. But what of the occasional multi-party cases in which the current speaker *does* laugh first? The following section reviews and offers accounts for some of these exceptional instances.

When current speaker laughs first

The few multi-party instances in which current speaker does initiate shared laughter are distinguished by the nature of their laughables. These derive their laughability from some other source than current speaker (laughable producer), or assign credit for the laughter to someone other than current speaker. They contrast to those laughables arguably designed to draw volunteered recipient laughter, with "ownership" of the laughable and credit for the laughter going to current speaker. One such case happens to follow immediately the instance just described. Recall that Stanley and Sondra began by teasing Jerry about not having a woman but rather sleeping all day. Stanley then turned the talk to a teasing sexual innuendo about Sondra and Jerry. They laugh together at this tease:

(UTCL A30a)

STAN	She sai'ya sl<u>ee</u>p all day ma:n?
	(1.6)
STAN	She c<u>ou</u>ld be.
	(1.5)
STAN	No woh won' say that,
SONDRA	uh₍-h! hheh heh heh heh₍-heh •hh
JERRY	[eh teh (.)heh-h↑ih heh-h↑ih]

The shared laughter subsides and a gap follows. Jerry marks the command to "ease up" as comical by repeating it three times, then twice more. Stanley produces what may be appreciative metatalk about this moment then a comical assessment of Jerry as a "poor boy." Another gap follows.

	(0.9)
JERRY	<u>Ea</u>se up. E ₍ase up. <u>Ease</u>₍ up
STAN	[(dz) Y<u>e</u>::::.] u::::'ow you
	gonna ack₍ a b o u' i t. ₍
JERRY	[Ease up ease up.]
STAN	Poor bo:y
	(0.6)

Stanley asks the others what they would do without him. Following this utterance Stanley initiates shared laughter and Jerry ratifies it:

STAN	Whuhwudjyou do without me.
STAN	ihh h₍ nh h↑ih₍ uh!
JERRY	[nhh! [
( )	[°•uih::::::uk •ehh°

Thus Stanley produces two sequentially tied, proximate laughables: one a tease, the other an apparent reference to himself as previous laughable-producer. The first time, another speaker laughs first; the second time, Stanley does. One difference may lie in the nature of the two laughable utterances. The first sets up two warrants for recipients (and not the current speaker) to laugh. It is constructed as one person teasing two; thus the two are cast together and can laugh together to display like-mindedness. In addition, the laughable invites the hearers to display understanding (awareness) of its possible sexual innuendo. The subsequent laughable ("what would you do without me") invites all three speakers to show like-mindedness towards the prior talk – that it is not to be taken seriously – and towards Stanley. Hence by initiating shared laughter Stanley offers a display of alignment with Jerry and Sondra. Furthermore, the latter laughable does not propose laughability solely on its own merits but by referring to himself as producer of the previous one. The first one already having drawn volunteered shared laughter from recipients, this one reinvokes the first and serves as a way to extend appreciation of it and its author.

A common feature runs through laughables in several of the exceptional multi-party cases. These laughables tend to be ones over which the current speaker does not claim authorship. They may, for example, be reporting someone else's original laughable actions or utterances. By initiating shared laughter, the current speaker invites others to share in appreciation of the laughable.

The next excerpt, shown earlier in this chapter, clearly illustrates the current speaker laughing first at an utterance she hearably does not "own." Carlin has gotten a surprise cake, song, and card in honor of her birthday. She is reading inscriptions from the card aloud. Ed prompts her to read more with "And I said what." Carlin reads Ed's inscription to her, containing an initial compliment, and a teasing insult:

(UTCL J2)

ED	And ↑I said wh<u>a</u>t.
	(3.0)
CARLIN	Sweet and k<u>i</u>:nd.
	(0.7)
(JAN)	°(iy)A<u>w</u>::hh°
	(1.2)
CARLIN	<u>Y</u>ankee

Following the "Yankee" reference Carlin initiates laughter with which Jan joins:

| CARLIN | <u>Y</u>ankee ehh-h<u>e</u>h h<u>a</u>h ↑hah hah₍ °huh-huh°₎ |
| JAN | ₍eh h<u>i</u>h ₎ hih h<u>i</u>h hih |

That this laughable was created by Ed is available to the participants. Although Carlin is current speaker, the laughable-producer is co-present and claims ownership of it. By laughing first Carlin does not violate a norm against self-praise, since this hearably is not her laughable but Ed's. In fact, since she is the butt of the teasing inscription, her first laugh may be even more strongly relevant, displaying for the others that she takes the laughable as non-serious and has not, for example, gotten her feelings hurt.

In summary, current speakers do sometimes start shared laughter. In these cases, a current speaker may not hearably claim authorship of the laughable, or the laughable may derive its laughability not from its own features but by reinvoking some other laughable. Such cases do not conform to a more general participant bias against the current speaker initiating shared laughter in multi-party settings, but they may display participant orientation that this general bias may be relaxed in the production of certain kinds of laughables.

Two-party shared laughter: current speaker laughs first

Contrasting to the multi-party situations shown above, in two-party interactions the most common case is for the current speaker to laugh first when shared laughter occurs. In attempting to account for this distributional difference, I have examined a variety of multi-party shared laugh instances, tracking how participant alignments and orientations to the laughable may be displayed. I have argued that when current speakers produce laughables for which they might take credit, laughing first serves as self-praise which speakers may avoid. In two-party interactions, however, self-laughter is unavoidable if shared laughter is to occur. It may be then that norms against self-laughter get relaxed somewhat. Among the two-party instances in the data, some show the current speaker laughing first at what participants treat as an intendedly funny laughable for which that person might claim credit. Other kinds of laughables for which current speakers laugh first include self-deprecation, attributed laughables, and those marking the utterance as not serious.

The current speaker may produce a laughable that self deprecates. In such a case, laughing first invites the other to laugh along *at* the current speaker. In the instance below, Ida's utterance offers a self-deprecating assessment of her house as "filthy." By this laughable plus within-speech laugh particle Ida invites laughter at herself. Jenny joins in shared laughter, while neither agreeing with nor disconfirming the assessment:

(Rah:II:24)

```
4       IDA         My house is filthy J(h)en⌊ny
5       JENNY                        ⌈hhhheh-•hhehh
```

Speakers can repeat or reconstruct talk specifically attributed to someone else. In such a case, the current speaker laughing first displays appreciation of that item while assigning "authorship" for it elsewhere. In the excerpt below, Kate has recounted to Brandon her father's tall tale that she was born in a pumpkin patch. She continues the retelling, here in regards to her sister:

(UTCL D6)

```
        KATE        Patty was found under a
                    ro(ho)ck ↑heh⌊ huh
        BRAND                ⌈eh (h)under a ro:ck.
```

Brandon repeats the phrase "under a rock" preceded by two brief laugh particles, ratifying Kate's shared laugh invitation. Prior talk makes Kate's utterance hearable as something told to her, rather than her own construction from original materials. Thus her laughter displays appreciation not of her own humor, but someone else's, which she retells.

Third, current speakers will laugh first to mark the laughable as "not-serious"; that is, not carrying its usual sequential implications. Here, emphasis is not on a clever jibe or humorous production which might bring credit to the originator or performer; rather, it is to disambiguate a turn for which hearers determining whether the speaker is joking might shape relevant responses or not. In this instance, Ellen reports that a third party (to whom she switched briefly via call waiting) says "hi" to Melody. Melody says she doesn't remember the person, and Ellen reminds Melody that they met at Ellen's birthday party. Melody's response – a flat "oh" with no recognition display – suggests that she does not remember Amy. After a pause, she produces a mock-disagreement over when the party occurred; its implication may be a complaint that she should not be expected to remember someone she met so long ago. She follows this with a brief, equivocal laugh particle. In replying, Ellen embeds one laugh particle, completing what may be the briefest possible occurrence of shared laughter:

(UTCL A20:HM1)

M E L O D Y	°Who's Amy Schreiner,°
E L L E N	•t ↑You m<u>e</u>t 'er:., coupla years ago. At-that- <u>b</u>irthday party?
	(0.6)
E L L E N	(I)-⌈ ⌉ <u>D</u>anielle had for me?
M E L O D Y	⌊Oh. ⌋
M E L O D Y	O::h.
	(1.0)
M E L O D Y	Ellen that was like (0.7) four years ag- no I'm kiddingh⌈ h
E L L E N	⌊I kno(h)w i's (.) >i'z a very long time ago.< But sh<u>e</u> remembers <u>you</u>:.

Taken "seriously," Melody's utterance proposes disagreement with Ellen over how long ago the party was and sanctioning of Ellen for expecting Melody to remember something that far past. The "no I'm kidding" plus brief laugh particle modify her utterance as a joke, not to be taken at face value. Sequentially, Ellen can respond to it as playful or laughable rather than, for instance, as an initiated repair sequence calling for subsequent revision of Ellen's prior turn, or as disagreement possibly calling for further disagreement. In this instance, a first laugh by the current speaker cues the other in the matter of how to respond to (and make sense of) the prior utterance.

In the following telephone conversation opening (although it is not the beginning of the phone call, having been preceded by another interaction), Rick's greeting shows exaggerated emphasis and intonational contour. He appends laugh particles to completion of this greeting. Cara does not laugh and her try-marked pronunciation of Rick's name suggests possible trouble identifying him from his voice sample. He repeats the greeting with lessened but still exaggerated contour, with laugh particles embedded. Cara produces a minimal second laugh plus an epithet and initial topic inquiry:

(UTCL D08a)

```
1    RICK     ↑ee↓YE:[ : ↑ E S ?   ]  hh huh heh heh=
2    (    )              [(Hey Ri:ck)]
3    CARA     =Ri:ck?
4    RICK     •ehhh. heYe(h)[es?
5    CARA                      [°hn° Yih quee:r w(h)at're y[a doin.]
6    RICK                                                    [•ehhh ]
```

By marking his greeting as not serious via delivery features and laughter, Rick proposes that this opening sequence not follow "ordinary" patterns. Rather than a first pair part greeting making relevant second pair part greeting, this play version of a greeting makes laughter, repair, and metatalk relevant.

First laugh by the current speaker may be particularly important for problematic or marginal laughables, the laughs providing clearer coding of the referred-to action or utterance. In the two examples shown here – a mild exaggeration of time (from two years to four) and a silly-voiced greeting which has already failed to draw recipient appreciation or co-participation – current speaker's first laugh marks the item as laughable. In each case, the other gives only the briefest of shared laughs before moving on.

In summary, three kinds of sequential activities seem associated with, and marked by, the current speaker laughing first in two-party conversations. The current speaker may produce laughables which self-deprecate or construct self as the butt of tease or story. Following these, first laughter displays willingness to laugh with other at self. The current speaker can recount a laughable attributed to someone else and laugh first. Finally, the current speaker may use first laugh to display that some action or utterance is laughable and thereby carries different sequential implications than if it were "serious."

For these activities, current speakers routinely choose to invite recipient laughter rather than, as an alternative, not laughing first and allowing hearers opportunities to volunteer laughter. In each case the current speaker's initial laugh proposes a treatment of the laughable and invites the recipient to align with the current speaker in that treatment. Thus, "current speaker laughs first" can be seen to be, in part, related to and reflecting the type of laughable to which it refers.

The preceding analysis points to a variety of local activities that speakers accomplish through initiating shared laughter. These activities, centering on orientation to laughable, orientation to co-participant, and cueing recipient for relevant next turn laughter, concern the immediate sequential environment. Yet the sequential workings of shared laughter also affect and reflect longer conversational episodes, and who laughs first may be understood in the light of deeper interactional considerations. The following case study demonstrates how local, sequential explanations for current speakers laughing first can co-exist with, and amplify, analyses of longer episodes of talk. By knowing what laughter displays and provides for, conversationalists can employ it at particular moments to accomplish interactional ends.

Case study: working through interactional difficulties

Earlier examples show current speakers initiating shared laughter and displaying willingness to laugh at self. In the following excerpt, the current speaker, Ida, laughs first after her utterance, and Jenny joins in:

(Rah:II:21. TS by G. Jefferson. They are talking about exercises. Ida says she tries to do a little bit every day.[5])

```
21:14    IDA        eh Not the floo:h one
14a                 ehh:: ⌈h⌊ euh he ⌈h-heh-he ⌈h
15       JENNY            ⌊ehh   ⌊he:h      ⌊he:h •kkhh •hn
```

Ida is older than Jenny, and her age in her exercise class has become a topic of talk here. In addition, she has described the exercise room (where her class meets) as cold. So this reference to avoiding floor exercises may orient to her age, the difficulty of the exercises, and/or to the cold floor. It shows a current speaker laughing *at* herself for being unwilling to do certain exercises. Ida invites Jenny to laugh along at Ida.

Speakers may use such a sequence – self-laughable, self-laughter, and other laughter – to extricate themselves from or remedy interactional difficulties. This sequence follows protracted, largely embedded negotiations over a possible invitation, and closely follows a sequence in which Ida extends an overt social invitation and Jenny declines by disattending. At such a moment, laughter may smooth over possible rupturing consequences of the declination and display affiliation among participants. Teasing oneself and inviting others to laugh along represents one way to bring about shared laughter, and thus can prove useful for achieving affiliative displays.

Ida introduces the topic of exercise a couple of minutes earlier in the conversation. She begins a new utterance marked as a suddenly remembered interjection into what might otherwise be the beginning of a narrative or description (line 24). Jenny provides a first pair part question relevant to Ida's prior turn but disattending the sudden-remembering marker:

(Rah:II:17. TS by G. Jefferson.)

```
17:24  IDA      Uh I went last Wednesdih yih know •hh
24a             Oh ↑by the wa:y=
25     JENNY    =Oh didche ↑keep fi:t,
```

A few turns later, Jenny asks if Ida was the only old person there. Ida replies that there are plenty of people older than she is. Jenny offers assessment of this news. Ida produces an alternative, upgraded assessment of the event (lines 8–9). Ida then continues with description of the exercise room:

(Rah:II:18. TS by G. Jefferson.)

```
18:7   JENNY    =Oh well thaht's
7a              a(hh)r ⌈(hh)ight th(h⌈ h)en  •a h  •a h⌉=
8      IDA             ⌊°•u  :  :  :° ⌋  (aout thehr) it's⌋
9      IDA      =⌈⌈↑ma⌉ hrvelou⌈ s.
10     JENNY    ⌈⌈•ah ⌉       ⌈•kh •hhe:hh
11     IDA                    ⌊becau:se . . .
```

Moments later, Ida produces another item mid-utterance that marks sudden remembrance and interjection of a thought (line 10). She does not continue this new thought but repeats the "marvelous" assessment, adding that the class is a "laugh":

(Rah:II:19. TS by G. Jefferson.)

```
19:9   JENNY    B⌈ 't I didn're⌈ alize that'⌉s wheh you w'going⌉
10     IDA      ⌊O h : : : : ⌈ I it's uh ⌉ Hey  (b') jih ⌉ know=
11     JENNY    =⌈⌈Mm:,
12     IDA      ⌊⌊eh Jenny it's marhrv'lous ah- u ↑LAU:gh wWe:ll.
```

Ida has twice done sudden remembering, and these may attempt to
shift from talk about the last exercise class to an invitation to attend the next one. Ida now reports that Jano (her daughter) told
Ida to attend because there would be other older people there.
This provides another possible opening for Ida to invite Jenny
or for Jenny to indicate interest in attending. Jenny rather pursues the age topic via a laughable contrasting Ida to the younger
participants:

(Rah:II:19. TS by G. Jefferson.)

```
19:15  IDA     Well ah think thahss why Jano said ↑yes c'm on
16             Ma b'coss she knew theh wuh lohds olduh
16a            ⌈th'n  ⌈me (et that                        )
17     JENNY   ⌊•hh  ⌊Ah: well thaht's awright then a(h)h
18             th(h)ought you might be theah with all thih
19             young swingihs yih⌈ nehhh heh⌉ heh⌉ •khu:⌉=
20     IDA                       ⌊ O o : h  ⌋ no:⌋ Oh n-⌋
```

After providing more description, Ida explicitly invites Jenny to join
them at exercise class. She delivers the invitation with a "smile voice"
(indicated on the transcript by the bracketing "£" signs) and attributes the invitation to Jano. Jenny responds with the token "Oh"
plus laughter. This laughter may display Jenny treating the invitation to exercise as "not serious"; i.e., not requiring a hearable second
pair part response. She neither accepts nor declines the invitation to
exercise:

(Rah:II:20. TS by G. Jefferson.)

```
20:23  IDA     An' ih eh-ih ahs Jano said, if evuh you
24             wanted tih cuu:m you £cuum£ Jenny,
25     JENNY   eOh:?hhh heh heh •eh h:     •h h h i : h
```

Jenny has treated the invitation as laughable and not serious.
Ida now retroactively displays the invitation as sequentially serious –
that is, making relevant that Jenny "seriously" accept or decline – via
the term "honestly." She adds more information relevant to inviting,
repeating an earlier positive assessment and adding that it is only an
hour and that they got back promptly:

(Rah:II:20–21. TS by G. Jefferson.)

```
20:25   JENNY   eOh:?hhh ⌈heh heh⌉ •eh⌉ h: •h h h i:h ⌉
26      IDA              ⌊Hon↑es'⌋ly  ⌊it's marhv'lous,⌋=
21:1    JENNY   =hn⌈ •hhh
2       IDA         ⌊It's only en hou:eh,
3                   (.)
4       JENNY   iYe⌈ :h,
5       IDA        ⌊From hahlf pahst eight to hahlf pahss ↓ni:ne.
6               •hh Em we were bahck here et twenty tuh te:n.
```

Jenny does not explicitly decline the invitation, yet she gives an account for declining: that it really doesn't do any good unless one
goes every day, and she hasn't been going. Accounts routinely accompany dispreferred actions (Levinson, 1983, p. 334), and that
regularity might incline Ida to hear this as declination. Ida agrees
with Jenny's statement:

(Rah:II:21. TS by G. Jefferson.)

```
21:7    JENNY   •hh (W'l) it mekshu feel bett'r if yih do a
8               little exihcise b't really you w'd need t'do it
9               ev'ry da:y don't you. This i⌈ s (the thi:ng.)⌉
10      IDA                                ⌊ Well u Y e : s ⌋=
```

Although Jenny has not declined the invitation, at this point it is
hearable that she is not inclined to accept it. Ida now moves away
from inviting by taking Jenny's preceding generalization and apply-
ing it to herself, that she tries to do a little bit every day. She then
produces a laughable utterance plus first laugh invitation, which
Jenny accepts with second laugh:

(Rah:II:21. TS by G. Jefferson.)

```
21:10   IDA     Well u Y e : s
11      IDA     Well (.) ah (.) try tih do a little bit e:v'ry
12              da:y, yih ⌈kno:w,⌉
13      JENNY             ⌊ i Ye:s,⌋
14      IDA     eh Not the floo:h one
14a             ehh:: h⌈ euh he⌈h-heh-he⌈h
15      JENNY         ⌊e hh  ⌊h e :h  ⌊he:h •kkhh •hn
```

Immediately after this shared laughter Ida opens up the closing
sequence (Schegloff and Sacks, 1984) of the conversation:

```
(Rah:II:21. TS by G. Jefferson.)
21:14   IDA        eh Not the floo:h one
14a                ehh:: h  euh he h-heh-he h
                        ⌊    ⌊         ⌊
15      JENNY           ⌈e hh   ⌈h e :h   ⌈he:h •kkhh ⌈•hn
16      IDA                                          ⌊I'll=
17                 ahftih ↓go:h Jenny . . .
```

Now, having traced the larger sequential environment in which
the sequence on lines 14–15 occurs, one can see how it appears
suited to these particular circumstances. Shared laughter displays affiliation, and its placement following the declined invitation makes
it useful in remedying possible interactional offense or face threat
arising out of the declination. Here, the shared laughter marks a
closing down of both topic and invitations. Ida's shared laugh initiation accomplishes at least two tasks – one locally sequential, the
other relevant to the longer episode and interactional displays. She
teases herself, for being old and for avoiding the cold floor, and
invites Jenny to laugh along at herself. Second, following the dis-
attended social invitation, her laughable plus first laugh provides
an opportunity for them to laugh together, affiliating momentarily,
before moving on to other matters.

Discussion

Most shared laughter in conversation begins with one person inviting another by laughing first. Variations in who laughs first allow
participants to display, orient to, and negotiate alignments towards
the laughable, each other and context. Starting from discussion of
the current-speaker – other distinction, this chapter has examined
the relevance of "number of parties" to the organization of who
laughs first. A statistical distribution indicates that in the vast majority of instances of two-party shared laughter, the current speaker
laughs first, while in the vast majority of multi-party instances, someone else laughs first. Analysis of particular instances points to several
factors that may contribute to this curious distribution. Participants
in multi-party interactions have an extra degree of freedom in their

choice among sequential roles of laughable-producer and laugher. One speaker may produce a laughable, while multiple others may laugh. The current speaker may then laugh after others have begun. When only two people are interacting, both must participate if shared laughter is to occur. Generally, one of the two will produce the laughable stimulus, and thus must laugh at his/her own materials if shared laughter is to occur.

Analysis of multi-party cases leads to the hypothesis that speakers may orient to a bias against the current speaker laughing first at laughables designed to draw volunteered recipient laughter while giving ownership (and credit) to the current speaker. In such cases, the current speaker laughing first could constitute a form of self-praise. A similar bias against self-praise seems to operate for other conversational features and for laughter in public settings, such as standup comedy. Other instances of shared laughter initiation appear as variations of this basic configuration. The current speaker may not orient to the turn-in-progress as laughable or may display orientation to other conversational features while refraining from initiating shared laughter. The exceptional multi-party cases in which current speakers do laugh first may reflect different sorts of laughables: the current speaker unwittingly produces a laughable (such as an error), gets teased, or produces a laughable in a way that avoids credit for it (e.g., attributing it to someone else).

In two-party shared laugh instances, the current speaker laughing first seems to reflect three different kinds of sequential activities. The current speaker may, as in exceptional multi-party cases reported above, avoid ownership for laughable. Second, the laughable may be one which self-deprecates, in which case laughing first would not be heard as self-praise but as willingness to laugh at self. Alternatively, the current speaker laughing first may accomplish marking as sequentially not serious an utterance or action. In such a case, first laugh both invites recipient to laugh along and cues recipient for what sort of next turn is relevant.

These issues point to the complexity of what initially might seem a rather simple and even trivial feature of social organization. The negotiation of "who laughs first" provides evidence for participant orientation to the nature of the laughable, relationship to co-participant(s), and sequential function within longer episodes of talk. The multi-party situation does seem to open up more possibilities for how people organize themselves in sequential roles of laughable-producer, laugher(s), and others. However, whether the current speaker or someone else laughs first may display more about relationship to laughable and each other and the kinds of interactional work getting done through laughter than it does simply about how many people are participating. A case study shows how one speaker in a two-party interaction laughs first at a self-deprecating laughable. She places that laughable plus laughter following a lengthy narrative description that several times hints at, and finally leads to, an invitation. Her interlocutor consistently resists topical movement towards the invitation. When the invitation finally does arrive, the interlocutor quickly declines. Placed immediately following invitation and declination, the laughable plus laughter provide resources for participants to align in the wake of possible rupture of relationship. Laughing at oneself tactfully gets shared laughter going without risking further rupture as might, for example, a tease of the other. Laughter may display affiliation with or disaffiliation from others. Which, if either, of these it contributes to is a matter worked out in interaction. How participants accomplish laughing *at* and laughing *with* is the focus of the next chapter.

5

Laughing at and *laughing with*: negotiating participant alignments

We think of laughter as an occasionally risky pleasure, like sex, which is a good thing in itself, or at least when done in the right way and kept in its place. (de Sousa, 1987, p. 228)

The phrases *laughing at* and *laughing with* suggest a long-recognized distinction between the power of laughter to promote distancing, disparagement, and feelings of superiority; or, conversely, to promote bonding and affiliation (see Chapter 1). Within CA research, Jefferson (1972) proposes (in passing) laughing at versus laughing with as a distinction to which participants orient. More recently, Clayman (1992) analyzed the affiliative status of audience laughter during the televised 1988 US presidential debates. Out of a total of 174 audience laughs in three different debates, Clayman codes twenty-four as "disaffiliative." Of these, twelve are "disaffiliative laughter" and four are "equivocal laughter." Affiliative laughter tends to follow (and refer to) one speaker's criticisms of his/her opponent – criticisms which are marked as humorous through such devices as warning that a joke is coming; using far-fetched, metaphorical descriptions; and employing fillers and hesitations after the laughable to allow turn space for the anticipated response by the audience. Disaffiliative laughter occurs following positive self-talk by a candidate (including descriptions or assessments of speakers' own qualities and accomplishments); and in such a context laughter can be heard as treating positive self-praise as "not-serious." Clayman's study demonstrates that analysts (like participants) must look to features of the local sequential environment to disambiguate laughter's status as affiliative or disaffiliative.

Four keys, which may be present in any laugh-relevant sequential context, help distinguish laughing at from laughing with: the laughable, first laugh, (possible) second laugh, and subsequent activities. After explaining each and showing how configurations of the four display *laughing at*, I will present cases where participants effect transformations from *with* to *at* or *at* to *with*.

Keys to distinguishing *laughing at* from *laughing with*

1. Laughable. Of the broad class of conversational laughables (including any object that serves as a referent for laughter), certain types appear likely to make *laughing at* relevant. Specifically, in *laughing at* environments, the *laughable appoints/nominates some co-present as a butt*. Participants may act as perpetrators of such laughables by ridiculing, teasing, or making fun of co-present others. The butt may collaborate in this alignment, even in the absence of perpetration, by producing overbuilt turns that make teasing relevant (Drew, 1987), errors (Hopper and Glenn, 1994), unintentional double entendres, talk or actions revealing a naive or otherwise sanctionable state, etc. Thus the laughable that nominates some co-present as a butt may be produced by that person or by someone else as perpetrator.

   2. First laugh. *First laugh by someone other than the butt (especially by perpetrator) likely indicates laughing at.* Current speaker invites recipient laughter by *laughing with*in or following the current utterance (see Chapter 3). Following a laughable that nominates a co-present as butt, first laugh by someone other than the nominated butt of the laughable provides additional confirmation that it is a *laughing at* environment. This first laugh may come from current speaker, especially if current speaker produces the laughable that identifies someone else as butt.

   3. (Possible) second laugh. *In multi-party interactions, (possible) second laugh by someone other than butt reinforces laughing at. In two-party situations, laughing at is not shared.* Thus two-party shared laughter will likely be a *laughing with*, while multi-party laughter may be *laughing with* or *laughing at*.

   4. Subsequent activities. *Subsequent talk on topic displays laughter as at.* Whether laughter is at or with may depend on retroactive definition through subsequent activities. One such activity (Jefferson, 1972, pp. 300–301) involves extending the topic through word or phrase repetitions. Repetition of another speaker's prior talk plus laugh tokens can be a way of appreciating something just said.

In some cases repeat + laughter does get followed by attempts to continue topic talk. Here, laughter's ambiguity becomes relevant. If laughter is *with*, that is, appreciating, then it will function as a terminator. If the laughter is *at* – disaffiliative – it functions, like a questioning-repeat, to produce more talk, perhaps including a repair, of the trouble item. Delay followed by repeat may show participant uncertainty about which meaning of laughter is in operation. The attempt to continue the topic gives more chances to resolve that ambiguity.

Jefferson (1972, p. 301) further suggests that these alternatives are not symmetrical – rather, there exists a "uni-directionality" to them such that *laughing at* is unambiguously hearable as such, while *laughing with* may also be *laughing at*. Even when one speaker does something specifically to be funny, there is the possibility that hearers may laugh, not for the reasons speaker wants, but for reasons carrying some degree of judgment or criticism of the speaker.

The following exemplifies how these features combine to display a clear instance of *laughing at*. Kate tells Brandon to forget about the tape recorder (which is recording them). After several exchanges during which he remains silent, she goes on to construct a tease:

(UTCL D6a)

```
1→      KATE      Betchyou sound really stupid on tape too.
                  (2.0)
2→      KATE      ₍₎ Bhh hah ↑huh huh ₎ °•hh°=
(3→)    BRAND     ⁽⁽ Do ↑I soun' stupid? ⁾
        KATE      =I betcha do:.
4→      BRAND     Yeah: ↑I've heard myself before ↑I sound
                  pretty °stupid.°
                  (.)
        KATE      W'↑you sound pretty (.) stupid . . .
```

The #1 arrow marks the laughable which nominates Brandon as butt, providing an imagined assessment of how he sounds on tape recorder. After a silence, Kate provides first laugh (arrow #2). Simultaneously Brandon produces non-laughing talk; he does not share in Kate's laughter (arrow #3). This leads to subsequent talk on topic (arrow #4). The combination of cues – laughable which nominates a butt, first laugh by someone else (the perpetrator), butt not sharing laughter, and subsequent talk on topic – clearly displays this as an instance of *laughing at*.

These features provide a starting point for understanding some of the ways people may disambiguate *laughing at* from *with*. In the following section some more complex instances are presented, in which conversationalists transform situations from *laughing at* to *with* or *with* to *at*. Explication of these instances displays how *laughing at* and *with* are alignments to which participants orient; such explication will also show that these alignments are not fixed but changeable, sometimes equivocal, and subject to moment-by-moment negotiation.

Transforming *laughing with* to *laughing at*

Joke-telling would seem inherently to set up *laughing with* environments. The teller seeks recipient laughter, which one would expect would display affiliation among participants, appreciating the joke and the telling. However, joke-telling environments may be volatile. Tellers must deliver the joke successfully; hearers must "get" the joke and respond appropriately. Failure in either role may convert a *laughing with* context into a *laughing at*.

In the following instance, six people representing three generations of an extended American family are gathered in a kitchen, telling jokes. Milt brings a narrative joke to completion. The joke concerns a granddaughter and grandmother, and its humor turns on the child's naivety and on the declining sexual activity of older adults. Following the punch line Chris laughs (line 31) and Cecil adds an appreciative "oh no" with laugh particles (line 33). It is, at this point, a *laughing with* environment:

(SIUC NP)

27	MILT	Sh'aid (for-) a:bso↑lutely right. (0.7) She says
28		I think I: know why you and grandpa sleep in
29		separate rooms.=Sh'said ↑Why is ↑that.
29a		Said you got an F in se:x.
30		(0.8)
31	CHRIS	Ohh HA HA H₁A HA HA HA₁ •↑Hooo=
33	CECIL	=↑Hoh ↓n:o.₁ •↑huuh

Overlapping Chris's laugh, Vaughn's repair initiator (line 32) asks for a repeat of the materials that follow "got a." The non-laughing question displays that Vaughn does not get the joke. But Milt does not (nor does anyone else) immediately provide the information Vaughn seeks, and Vaughn repeats the repair initiator (line 34).

```
31   CHRIS     Ohh HA HA H⌈ A    HA    HA    HA⌉ •↑Hooo=
32   VAUGHN              ⌊   Ya gotta what?  ⌋
33   CECIL     =↑Hoh ↓n:o.⌈ •↑huuh
34   VAUGHN               ⌊°Got a° what?
```

Milt, the joke-teller, now laughs (line 37). But placement of Milt's laugh suggests that it orients not to his own joke, but to Vaughn's questioning repair initiator. Evidence for this includes Milt's use of Vaughn's name, with laugh particles embedded in it, and his subsequent turn calling for someone to explain the joke to Vaughn (line 40). The joke's punch line provides an opportunity for the participants to align and laugh with each other. Now the others are invited to laugh with Milt *at* Vaughn. Although it is not clear from talk at this point whether others in the group *also* didn't hear or get the joke, Vaughn's repair initiators make clear that *he* doesn't understand.[1] For this demonstrated naivety, Vaughn gets laughed at:

```
34   VAUGHN    °Got a° what?
35             (0.3)
36   (?):      ↑•hu⌈ uh-huh
37   MILT        ⌊Va⌈ (hh)ughn?⌈  •hh yes ha ha ⌈ha h uh
38   CECIL         ⌊↑oh: ↑oh ⌊↑ohuh-hoo       ⌊↑•uhhh-=
39             =⌈⌈hoo
40   MILT       ⌊⌊Somebody explain that to him.
```

Vaughn's repair initiators (lines 32 and 34) suggest that the problem lies in failure to hear part of the punch line, rather than hearing it but not understanding its full meaning. Yet Milt, through his turn at line 40, treats this as a failure to "get" the joke. Such a failure makes hearer subject to teasing and ridicule. Sacks (1992, vol. 1, pp. 671–672) explains that

Jokes, and dirty jokes in particular, are constructed as "understanding tests." Not everyone supposably "gets" each joke, the getting involving achievement of its understanding, a failure to get being supposable as involving a failure to understand. Asserting understanding failures can then reveal, e.g., recipients' lack of sophistication, a matter that an appropriately placed laugh can otherwise conceal.

By this last utterance, Milt singles Vaughn out for ridicule, suggesting that someone, indeed anyone else in the room could explain this joke to Vaughn. More laughs follow from Milt and others, but not from Vaughn. Vaughn accounts for his failure to laugh (line 49), invoking "not hearing" as the source of trouble rather than, for example, hearing but not "getting" the innuendo in the joke – though orienting to his prior actions being sanctionable (and in this case, sanctioned). It thereby provides confirmation of the isolating actions performed by Milt's *laughing at* him:

40	MILT	Somebody expl<u>ai</u>n that to him.
41	(?)	°nh-h₍ uh°
42	MILT	⌈hu hah hah₍ hah hah hah hah
43	CECIL	ˡ↑hu::h-₍↓huh
44	(?)	⌈°↑huh hih-hih°=
45	(?)	=°↑uh-hunh!°
46	(?)	°hhh₍ ::::::°
47	ETHEL	ˡ↑O:h ↓no(h)o=
48	(?)	=₍₍ (ehih uheh) ₍
49	VAUGHN	⌈⌈I didn't hearˡthe ↑f<u>ir</u>st word.

At the punch line of a joke, especially a joke with dirty or naughty overtones, hearers have an opportunity to display their understanding by laughing in appreciation. In this example, the participants affiliate in appreciating the joke until one of them displays that he hasn't gotten it. Then the joke-teller makes this hearer's failure itself into a laughable, thus transforming the interactional environment from *laughing with* to *laughing at*.

Transforming *laughing at* to *laughing with*

As the prior example shows, alignments displayed through *laughing at* or with are not static but changeable, dependent upon moment-to-moment ratification or re-negotiation. One sort of change involves the butt – the person laughed at – attempting to shift participant alignment to a *laughing with* via subsequent activities.

In the following example three American college students are talking on the telephone. After a prior topic winds down, Stanley refers to an earlier conversation he had with the "fellas" at the dorm. Neither Jeffrey nor Rhonda speaks during several transition relevance places and gaps (not shown below). Stanley emphasizes the term "deeming" within his turn that refers to the co-present interactor, Rhonda, in the third person, in a playful-formal phrase, "a young lady."

(UTCL A30)

> STAN   But d<u>ee</u>ming that a young ↑lady's on the phone
>   wu' we won' disc<u>u</u>ss none u'th<u>et</u>.
>   (1.6)

This turn proposes that Jeffrey and Stanley, as the two males (and perhaps as the "we" who won't discuss), align apart from Rhonda, the "young lady." As such it may make relevant Jeffrey and Stanley *laughing with* each other, at Rhonda. However, following the gap, Jeffrey initiates a repair sequence by a repeat and first pair part question. Stanley's second pair part marks that he doesn't know the meaning of the word he has just used and accounts for his having employed it only because it is "catchy":

> JEFF   <u>Dee</u>ming. Now ↑wha' does ↓d<u>eem</u>⌈ing mean ma::n.
> STAN   ⌊eh
> STAN   D<u>ee</u>ming ↑I don't know ma:n ↑is jus'as jus uh
>   c<u>:</u>atchy w<u>o</u>:rd ma:n.

Overlapping this Jeffrey starts laughing. That this is a *laughing at* environment is hearable by the nature of the laughable (getting caught using a term one doesn't understand), by Jeffrey's other-initiation of laughter, by Stanley's withholding second laugh and Rhonda providing it, and by initiation of subsequent talk on topic:

> STAN   eh D<u>ee</u>ming ↑I don't know ma:n
>   ↑is jus⌈   'as jus uh c<u>:</u>atchy w<u>o</u>:rd ⌉ ma:n.
> JEFF   ⌈↑h<u>ih</u>-huh hu↑<u>AH</u>!   huh-hah!⌋
> RHON   °↑hih⌈ heh.°
> STAN   ⌊It don't fit sh<u>i</u>t.

This last turn by Stanley serves as a new laughable orienting to his prior word-error. This turn's laughability lies at least in part in its brevity, internal rhyme, and use of the expletive "shit." By this Stanley bids to transform the environment to *laughing with*. Rhonda laughs and Jeffrey provides appreciative talk. Stanley continues, with another laughable relevant to his use of "deeming":

```
STAN     It don't fit shit.
RHON     ihh⌐  huh   huh    •h::h⌐
JEFF         ⌐Wu'I tellyou what ma⌐ ::⌐ ::n.
STAN                                ⌐My English teachuh
STAN     be exin my ass on that. ↑Ev'ry time.=
```

Stanley produces comic characterizations of an English teacher deleting an item from a paper as if it were to be banished or decapitated. Jeffrey and Rhonda laugh. Stanley has now successfully converted a *laughing at* environment into a *laughing with*, realigning from an accidental producer of a teasable error into an intentional producer of comic accounts and narration. The realignment achieved, he proceeds with non-laughing talk on the same subject.

```
RHON     =°Who de⌐eming?°
STAN              ⌐Deemin',
         (0.2)
STAN     Oogh!   It don' fit.
         (0.7)
STAN     ⌐Off with ⌐it.
JEFF     ⌐(t'sh)  ⌐mh! hmhuh⌐mhuh.
RHON                       ⌐u-huh?=
STAN     =I'm like right oh kay?
         (1.8)
STAN     See ↑I got that from this white guy ma:n,
```

Errors – in this case mis-using a word and not knowing what it means – make relevant *laughing at*. The producer of an error can recover artfully, as does Stanley, and bring those laughing back into alignment with him.

Willingness to go along with, or even initiate, laughter at oneself provides potential payoffs in realigning towards affiliation. Once *laughing at* either is underway or relevant, willingness to laugh at

self provides a resource for converting the environment to *laughing
with*.

By transforming *laughing at* to *with* (or vice versa), participants
may accomplish a micro-transformation of social structure. In his
autobiography, professional comedian Dick Gregory describes how
he did this as a child:

> I got picked on a lot around the neighborhood. . . . I guess that's when
> I first began to learn about humor, the power of a joke. . . . At first . . . I'd
> just get mad and run home and cry when the kids started. And then, I don't
> know just when, I started to figure it out. They were going to laugh anyway,
> but if I made the jokes they'd laugh *with* me instead of at me. I'd get the
> kids off my back, on my side. So I'd come off that porch talking about
> myself. . . .
>
> Before they could get going, I'd knock it out first, fast, knock out those
> jokes so they wouldn't have time to set and climb all over me. . . . And they
> started to come over and listen to me, they'd see me coming and crowd
> around me on the corner. . . .
>
> Everything began to change then. . . . The kids began to expect to hear
> funny things from me, and after a while I could say anything I wanted. I
> got a reputation as a funny man. And then I started to turn the jokes on
> them. (Gregory, 1964, pp. 54–55)

Gregory realigned his role from that of unwilling butt to willing
creator of jokes, from others *laughing at* him to *laughing with* and,
ultimately, to him *laughing at* others.

Knowledge of this possibility itself provides a resource for creating affiliation. Conversationalists can create situations in which
laughing at them is relevant, as a means of inviting and promoting
affiliation. One phrase in our common parlance for this is "playing the fool." Those who provide this role may begin as victims,
like Dick Gregory, or begin by willingly producing items for others
to laugh at. In ongoing relationships, who is to say which comes
first? Does Stanley, in the example above, play the fool because his
friends laughed at him? Or do his friends orient to the *possibility* of
laughing at him because he has, at other times, willingly played the
fool? Either way, *laughing at* and *laughing with* provide tools for
disaffiliating and affiliating.

With this discussion of affiliation and disaffiliation we have progressed from observations about the sequential organization of
laughter to interpreting how people create, modify, and maintain

social relationships through laughter and related phenomena. Focusing more on its affiliative workings, we move now to considering how laughter, and shared laughter, may contribute to displays of relational intimacy. At the same time, laughter contributes to the framing of play, and these accomplishments turn out to be closely connected.

6

Laughing along, resisting: constituting relationship and identity

Earlier chapters have shown the ways laughs are organized relative to speech and activity. In this chapter the focus moves to two distinct but connected sequential activities, and how these activities help people accomplish in-the-moment relationship and identity. One activity is *laughing along*. In response to teases and improprieties, laughter shows willingness to go along but (by itself) stops short of outright affiliation with what is going on. However, laughing along may well lead the recipient to being implicated further in activities in which that person is the butt of a tease or is invited to participate in potentially rude and offensive talk. This leads to the second sequential activity of interest in this chapter, *resisting*. Recipient laughter can show appreciation only, or even reluctance, rather than affiliation with what the laughable is doing. Laughing then offers a response somewhere between outright rejection and outright co-implication in potentially problematic talk.

This consideration of laughing along and resisting has its roots in two previous articles, and detailed explication of their arguments will help lay groundwork for the rest of the chapter. Drew (1987) shows how laughter occurs as a midpoint in a range of responses by the victims of teases. Similarly, Jefferson, Sacks, and Schegloff (1987) characterize laughter as occupying a midplace on a continuum of responses to improprieties and contributing to expanded sequences culminating in displays of intimacy. These articles establish grounds for showing how laughter affiliates with potentially volatile laughables and thus may implicate the laugher in those very activities. At the same time, laughter offers a basis for resisting the activities, not overtly as may be done through other means, but subtly in ways that perhaps maintain some affiliation. Through these possibilities, we can begin to appreciate the power of laughter in contributing to relationship and identity. Following reviews of the articles by Drew and by Jefferson, Schegloff, and Sacks, I will present two case studies, extending both analyses to consider issues of relationship and identity. In the first, laughter in response to teases and sexual innuendo helps build a flirtatious encounter. In the second, a recipient of teasing sexual innuendo first laughs along and then resists through features of her laughter. The chapter closes with a discussion of the laughter–gender connection. I will argue that the laughing along-while-resisting strategy is one commonly associated with women responding to sexual overtures from men, and that it offers evidence that people orient to gender in the sequential organization of laughter. Questions of whether, and how, participant orientation to gender might be empirically documented are situated within ongoing scholarly debates about approaches to studying gender and communication and about tracing connections between texts and contexts.

Laughter and teasing

As a response to being teased, laughter shows willingness to acknowledge humorous elements, even if taking the substance of the tease seriously. It stands as a middle-range response between rejection and going along. Teasing is inherently dualistic, containing both serious and playful elements (though individual teases may lean more heavily towards one or the other). The most comprehensive CA study of teasing is by Drew (1987). In about one-third of Drew's collection of teasing instances, the "victims" orient to the nonseriousness of the tease, usually by laughing. The victims of teases, Drew shows, respond in a number of ways which may be arrayed on a continuum in terms of their orientation to the laughable element, from non-laughing to laughing but responding seriously to "going along" and even escalating the teasable element. At one end are responses which treat the tease utterly seriously; these are what Drew terms "po-faced" receipts.

(Goodwin: Family dinner: 1, in Drew, 1987, p. 221)

DOT   Do we have two forks 'cause we're on
             television?

```
MOTHER    ₁No we-
ANGIE     ⌈huh huh   ₁huh  hh₁ h ( )
FATHER              ⌈Yeahah ⌈h hah •hh=
MOTHER                        uh huh  ₁huh huh
ANGIE                                ⌈heh heh heh
FATHER                                   ⌈=Right yeh
          Pro₁bably the answer right (the₁re)
ANGIE     ⌈eh hah hah                        ₁
MOTHER    You have pie:: tonight.        ⌈•hhh You have pie
```

Next on the continuum are responses in which the victims laugh
while at the same time rejecting what the tease proposes about them.
For example, in line 19 Lynn laughingly teases Beth about her preceding opinion. Beth provides a minimal laugh particle in the word
"We(hh)ll" while defending herself.

(SAA: BL, in Armstrong, 1992, p. 138)

```
16   B        You know (0.2) it c'n ↑either stay hot or it
17            could stay co:↓ld but-
18            (1.8)
19   L        Well now that's a pro↓fou(hh)nd ↓sta(h)temen(hh)
20   B        We(hh)ll (.) I mean like >if it gets< ho:t?
21            ↓it's gonna stay hot and never cool do:wn?=>but
22            if it's< (.) you know if it's ↑coo:l it's always
23            cool.=D'ju notice?
```

Third are instances in which victims first laugh, then separately
reject the teasing element, as Roger does in the following.

(GTS:I:1:44: R:7, in Drew, 1987, p. 223)

```
        LOUISE    What do you do to make yourself distinct=
        ROGER     =I mu- I must do something ₁I mean 'c₁ ause
        LOUISE                               ⌈Mmhm  ⌈You do,
        ROGER     ehhh hh ₁n hn
        AL               ⌈You JA:CK off in your chai:r
→       ROGER     ehh heh •hehh Ya:h •hnff•hh
                  (.)
→       ROGER     No everybody: (.) you know: looks for this
                  distinction.
```

Fourth, at the extreme nonserious end of the continuum, the victim does not reject the tease but actually goes along with it. This can be done by laughing only or by laughing and playing along, actually extending the tease against oneself. In the following example, Stan teasingly challenges Dave's account that he (cannot go out because he) must study for an exam. In response, Dave completely reverses his position such that he agrees with Stan's challenge.

(SIUC S1)

1	DAVE	I'm in Bart's room.
2	STAN	What are you doin' tonigh, hh
3	DAVE	↑Uh::hhh ↓I don'know man I gotta study for
4		that test.
5	STAN	You ain't got no damn test.
6	DAVE	•ehh Yeah I'm gonna go out an' get baked an'
7		drink 'n nhhh⌊ ⌊• uhh •uhh •uhh •uh
8	STAN	⌈heh hah ⌈ (• e u h h)

Because laughter can accompany rejection or acceptance of a tease, its presence does not necessarily indicate co-implication in what is being proposed. Rather, its job is to display appreciation, not affiliation. A clearer display might occur if recipient, in the context of shared laughter, produces next laughables that go along with the teasing and extend the shared laughter.

Teasing can occur in response to, and exploit, a variety of features of preceding talk. For instance, Drew (1987, p. 32) suggests that a prior speaker who gets teased often is "overdoing" something: not just complaining, but complaining excessively; not just telling any story, but an impossible one; and so on. Errors of fact or speech, social blunders, or displays of naivety provide other bases for teasing (see Chapter 5, and Armstrong, 1992). Hearers routinely let such items pass without notice, but another option is to treat them as teasable. In the following example, Beth repeats Lynn's statement with an added phrase and try-marked questioning intonation, in response to which Lynn teasingly corrects her and laughs:

(SAA: BL, in Armstrong, 1992, p. 45. They are talking about Mary Shelley)

	LYNN	She was thr<u>ee</u> years ↓younger than <u>Kea</u>ts.
		(("whistling noise))

BETH   ↑Thr<u>ee</u> >years yo<u>ung</u>er ↓than< Keats ↑when
            she died?
            (0.5)
BETH   ↓No.
            (0.5)
LYNN   Not when she di:<u>e</u>d, when she was <u>born</u>. Unih
            hnh hnh ha •hh

The continuum of responses to a tease may actually appear sequentially in the same instance. In the following, S teases T for her description of the weapons possessed by members of an urban street gang. The first tease consists of repeating the word "missiles" with laughter (which is also a standard format for a next turn repair initiator: see Schegloff, Jefferson, and Sacks, 1977). T disattends it and continues with a "po-faced" continuation of her description:

(CY.SIU.NS.011, TS 1995 by N. Stucky)

T   bl<u>a</u>ck shirts and black pants and (.) sku:ll caps on
            they face and stuff and they (.) ridin around here
            sh<u>oo</u>tin' up each other and with techni::nes and I
            mean missiles automaₜtics-
S   ˻mi(h)ssiles haₜ ha ha
T   ˻<u>oo</u>zies

S repeats the word "automatic," embedding laugh particles, and adding the phrase "nuclear weapons"; by this she teases a second time and provides a second opportunity for T to laugh along. T now acknowledges the tease (ok<u>ay</u>::.) but does not laugh. In overlap with S's continued laughter, T counterteases, accusing S of "bullshitting":

S   mi(h)ssiles haₜ ha ha
T   ˻<u>oo</u>zies
S   au(h)tomatic nu(h)clearweapons(h)
T   ok<u>ay</u>::.
S   haₜ hyuk
T   ˻Bush ain't got nothin on them while
            ya bu::llshittin'

S continues merrily on her way, adding more items to her *reductio ad absurdum* list of gang weapons, teasing T. This third opportunity brings laughter from T; immediately thereafter, S abandons the teasing to assess (comically) President Bush (Sr.):

T	⌈Bush ain't got nothin on them while ya bu:⌈:llshittin'
S	⌈ground ta air m⌈issiles
T	⌈uh- ha ha ha ha huh.
S	I me⌈an I'm like man
T	⌈and Bush ain't nothin but a block head son of a bitch any how huh

In summary, Drew's analysis shows laughter as a midpoint response to teases. It neither absolutely rejects nor co-implicates in the teasing mentality, but may be part of either. In the case just shown, teaser pursues recipient's laughter through repeated jests. For the recipient, the choice to laugh means abandoning the "serious" pursuit of topic and showing appreciation of the jests. Laughing, then, while not fully co-implicating, paves the way for pursuing the teaser's activity. We now turn to another environment in which laughing along plays a similar role.

Laughter and the expanded affiliative sequence; intimacy

Participants sometimes produce words or actions that might be considered breaches of ethics, tact, or courtesy (Jefferson, Sacks, and Schegloff, 1987, p. 160), such as rudeness or obscenity. A number of responses become relevant following such *improprieties*. Jefferson, Sacks, and Schegloff arrange these formulations as ordered from least to most affiliative: (a) overt *disaffiliating* from the impropriety, (b) *declining to respond*, (c) *disattending* the impropriety while responding to some innocuous part of the utterance, (d) *appreciating* the impropriety with laughter and/or talk, (e) *affiliating* with the impropriety by replicating it in a next utterance, and (f) *escalating* with a new impropriety. Laughter represents a midpoint on this continuum of disaffiliation to escalation. While laughter can show recipient's appreciation of the impropriety, when produced on its own without other verbal response, its stance towards the laughable is equivocal; e.g., a recipient's laugh might be derisive, appreciative, or embarrassed. In combination with talk, laughter might display different degrees of alignment with the offensive item. A more unequivocal display of co-implication occurs if recipient produces laughter plus a next impropriety.

Sometimes, a recipient directly affiliates with the impropriety by producing a similar item in the next turn, without need for laughter or repeated invitations. In the instance below, Stan uses the vulgar "wool" to refer to attractive females. Stan agrees with the assessment and produces a synonym, "coot":

(SIUC S1)

39	DAVE	There's a lot of wool at weddings.=Y'know that?=
40	STAN	=I know.=You wouldn't believe all the coot that
41		was up there.

In contrast to this pattern, Jefferson, Sacks and Schegloff note that some instances reflect a *progression* of responses to several consecutive potentially taboo topic approaches. In these, the recipient of an impropriety begins by resisting and then, in response to repeated offers, comes to show appreciation and affiliation. The basic sequence of impropriety → affiliation expands to the more complex pattern of impropriety → resistance → shared laughter → affiliation. The following excerpt shows such a trajectory. Gene produces an impropriety in line 3. Maggie acknowledges but provides no uptake on the possible offensive/problematic implications of "syphletic." Gene provides a laugh invitation, which Maggie accepts (lines 4–6). Following this, Maggie affiliates by offering a next laughable (line 7). This draws more laughter, then they move to serious talk on topic:

(Goldberg:II:1:2:1, in Jefferson, Sacks, and Schegloff, 1987, pp. 163–164)

1	GENE	Are yih avoiding me like the plague,=
2	MAGGIE	=nNo::: of wahl yih nah you know better th'n
2a		⌈t h a t⌉
3	GENE	⌊I'm <u>not</u>⌋ syp<u>hl</u>etic,=
4	MAGGIE	=•hhh <u>No</u>⌈ I know yer no⌊ t, h h h h ⌈•h h ⌉
5	GENE	⌊( ) ⌊heh, he-heh ⌋-heh-⌋
5a		heh-heh-⌈heh-⌈heh⌉
6	MAGGIE	⌊h h ⌊heh⌋ heh huh=
7	MAGGIE	=•hhhhhh ⌈I keep running te:sts onyuh I know
8	GENE	⌊( )
8a	MAGGIE	yer not.=

```
9    GENE     =ehh he- ⌈heh-heh-heh-heh-heh ⌉  °hn°=
10   MAGGIE            ⌊•h h h h h h         ⌋
11   MAGGIE   =UH::hhhhhhhh No Gene I've just hh •hhhhhh been
12            in en been out'n sometimes hhh y'know the pa:ths
13            •hhh cro:ss, bu:t uh th'ti:me is ba:d,
14            (0.7)
15   GENE     Ye:h. What's happ'ning
```

Similarly in the following extract, an initial impropriety receives disattention. A next version of it brings reciprocated impropriety. Immediately following, the first offerer laughs and escalates to a next impropriety. Both speakers then fully participate in improprieties and shared laughter. T's first impropriety (line 35) takes the form of an assessment of Melissa. W's response (line 36) is a minimal token which is ambiguous as to whether it is agreeing or merely acknowledging the assessment.

(SDCL: Two guys, in Beach, 2000, p. 382. W is telling a story about Melissa, who is his "little sister" via his fraternity and her sorority.)

```
30   W    >And she comes back like,< ↑How do I lo:ok:.=
31        =I'm like <o:h no:!>
32        £Like •hh£ let's not- £l(h)et's not start this
33        off on the wr(h)o::ng foo:t,=ya know?£
34        •hhh(sf) (.) So anyw ⌈ a:ys, ⌉
35   T                         ⌊>I do⌋n't think she's that
36        good loo:king do you?<=
37   W    =°Hm um.° (hh)
```

T pursues with another assessment, more sexual and potentially offensive than the previous one. W now affiliates by producing a next impropriety of his own:

```
38        (0.2)
39   T    >Sh:e'(s) got a nice litt:le- bo:dy<
40        ⌈↓°but that's ab out it.°⌉=
41   W    ⌊Mm:        h:m:,   ⌋
42   W    =pt>(We-) an' she got cute little breasts. <
```

T laughs briefly in overlap with the end of W's assessment and then escalates through a mock-Southern accent and an assessment of Melissa which invokes and then declines the possibility of doing her violence. In overlap with T's subsequent lengthy laugh stream, W affiliates and escalates with another impropriety. After extended laughing together, W resumes his story (line 58):

```
42   W    =pt>(We-) an' she got cute little br₁easts.  ₁ <
43   T                                    >£⌈Hu-•hh⌉h
44        I AIN'T GO'N- KI:LL 'ER!£<
45        He(g)h:::₁= ↑heh heh heh heh heh ↓hah hah hah₁
46   W          ⌈(D)a:mn ri::ght. £p(h)mph£ ↓If the    ⌉=
47   T        ₁hah hah hah₁
48   W    =⌈opportu- the⌉
49   W    opportunity did ar:i:se, but=
50   T    =U:h:=m:? ₁(h)m::₁,
51   W              =⌈nothin⌉ e:lse? did.=
52   T    =Ha ha ↑HA::H £But nothing else ro₁ se₁.£=
53   W                                    ⌈•hh⌉
54   W    =₁Heh ha:h ha:h ha- ha- (eghk eghk eghk eghk)
55   T    =⌈>Ha ha ha ha ha ha ha ha ha ha ha ha ha
56        •ih:gh::!< (.)O::₁  gh-  o:::h,  ₁b: a:d.=
57   W                ⌈O::hh my £Go:::d.⌉£
58   W    =But anyways, £s-huh huh.£> •hh So anyways
59        we go to In n' Out ((continues))
```

Laughter plays a role in these "expanded affiliative sequences" by providing a systematic basis for moving talk forward to a moment of co-implication. In the environment of an impropriety followed by laughter a warrant exists for participants to produce a next laughable as a means of providing for extended laughter. Since the previous laughable was an impropriety, then next laughable legitimately can take the form of another impropriety. The original item now can be heard as the first in a series of laughables serving as the basis for a possible extension of laughter (see Chapter 4). Laughter thus serves to provide a ". . . matrix in which speech events implicating the recipient of a possible offense in the offensive mentality can be elicited and embedded without breaking the conversational surface" (Jefferson, Sacks, and Schegloff, 1977, p. 19). That is, recipient can introduce a next impropriety smoothly into the sequential environment constituted and supported by laughables and shared laughter.

Impropriety, while possibly constituting an interactional breach, may also be understood as showing *intimacy*: "That is, the introduction of such talk can be seen as a display that speaker takes it that the current interaction is one in which he may produce such talk; i.e., is informal/intimate" (Jefferson, Sacks, and Schegloff, 1987, p. 160). If the presence of improprieties can mark a conversation as intimate, then by introducing such talk a speaker may initiate a move into intimate interaction. If so, then recipient not only may treat the acceptability of the impropriety itself, but also may treat it as an invitation to greater intimacy. The beginning point of this kind of sequence is the first introduction of an impropriety. Actions in subsequent turns provide opportunities for an intimacy display to follow.

These reviews show how in the wake of teases and improprieties, recipients employ a range of ways to respond, from serious and dis-affiliating, to laughing along, to affiliating and escalating. Laughing along itself does not necessarily affiliate, but it contributes to sequential environments in which affiliating becomes relevant. Common to both of these environments are risky laughables, possibly leading to hurt feelings or offense. Yet in that very riskiness lies a resource for bringing participants closer together. Lying at a crucial juncture in these sequences is recipient laughter. There are ways to resist directly, and these involve not laughing. Laughing along, while not outright affiliating, makes more of the same laughable (teasing or impropriety) relevant and may lead to clearer displays of affiliation. Yet in recipient laughter also lies the potential for resistance of a more subtle and ambiguous nature, and this will be explored later in this chapter. The following extended instance is intended to show how speech errors, teasing, shared laughter, and impropriety contribute to conversational play and intimacy.

Errors provide a potential basis for subsequent teasing and celebration. Shared laughter following an error provides a warrant for some next action to prolong the laughter (see discusison of extending shared laughter in Chapter 3, starting on p. 72), and the error itself becomes a potential extension device. That is, one error having served as a laughable, speakers can produce another, similar error, to provide for more shared laughs. Through more laughable errors and shared laughter, participants may frame their interaction as teasing or playful.

This excerpt occurs about eight minutes into a ten-minute conversation between two university students, one female and one male.

Evidence from elsewhere in their talk suggests that they are at least acquaintances, but that they are not (yet) deeply involved with each other sexually or romantically. After they have closed down a preceding topic, Rick initiates talk about dinner with a possible preliminary to an invitation (line 498). Cara responds that she has not had dinner, and asks if he has; this constrains him to continue on this topic with an answer and provides an opportunity for him to extend a dinner-related invitation. Instead he asserts his hunger, treating this disclosure as laughable:

(UTCL D8a)

```
498     RICK      Have you had dinner yet?
499               (0.6)
500     CARA      No I haven't. Have ⌈you,
501     RICK                         ⌊I- I'm so   h(h)ungry(h),
```

Cara produces a next question (line 502) which invites more talk from Rick on the topic of hunger and eating; her question also keeps open the possibility of Rick extending her a dinner invitation. Rick answers her question, and a gap follows. This provides another slot for an invitation, yet none is proffered. Cara produces another question (line 506) which continues talk on topic and keeps open the dinner possibility. However, this question contains a mistake in verb tense:

```
501     RICK      I- I'm so   h(h)ungry(h),
502     CARA      Are you starv⌈ing?
503     RICK                   ⌊°•eh°
504     RICK      ↑Ye:s.
505               (0.5)
506     CARA      Have you ate t'day?
```

Rick does not respond and a gap ensues. Cara corrects her own error by producing an amended verb, "eaten." The participants now could let the error pass and proceed with talk on the current topic (or something else). Instead, Rick laughs, initiating movement into playful treatment of her error:

```
506     CARA      Have you ate t'day?
507               (0.5)
508     CARA      Eat'n?
509     RICK      ehh heh-heh
```

Cara laughs along with Rick. Although brief, this shared laughter ratifies their co-orientation towards the error as laughable:

```
508   CARA      Eat'n?
509   RICK      ehh heh⌊ -heh
510   CARA            ⌈(d)↑Ay hay(huh)
```

Cara has already corrected the verb to its proper form. By now producing another improper version, with laughter, she provides them with an opportunity to continue laughing together. In effect, she willingly teases herself before Rick does any teasing:

```
510   CARA      (d)↑Ay hay(huh dub) £eated.
```

Cara's laugh tokens at 510 may be heard both as accepting Rick's invitation to laugh and marking her present turn as laughable. Hence the relevance of laughter is both *confirmed* and *forwarded* in Cara's line 510. As an alternate version of the problematic word, "£eated" fills the verb slot in her prior question. As a laughable, "£eated" invites recipient laughter from Rick. As an extension of the prior error-laughable, it proposes that they jointly produce more shared laughter and extensions. Thus Rick has several relevant next-turn options: he can answer the question, he can laugh, and/or he can produce a next laughable.

In his response he performs two of these three relevant next activities. He answers her question, replicating within his response her newest wrong verb-form. Then he follows his utterance – which forwards the laughter-relevance of the original error and its laugh-relevant re-playings – with laughter:

```
511   CARA      ↑•ehh⌊hh
512   RICK           ⌈No ↑I- I- I already eated. hh-hh-heh
```

Cara's next question provides Rick an opportunity to repeat, revise, or elaborate upon his answer. It also repeats his use of the error-form, 'eated.' After Rick's affirmative answer, Cara produces a follow-up question containing another incorrect grammatical form:

```
512   RICK      No ↑I- I- I already eated.⌊ hh-hh-heh
513   CARA                               ⌈You already eated?
514   RICK      Yes.
515   CARA      (Who) did jou eat at.   ehh! •hh
```

By this next laughable plus subsequent laughter she forwards the
continuing relevance of their laughing together. She also continues
the semblance of topic talk underlying the errors and laughs; that is,
"Where did you eat?" (a possible "correct" version of her question)
would provide a reasonable next question following "I've already
eaten." Abandoned, at least for the moment, is the possibility of
this talk leading to a dinner invitation, since "I've already eaten"
can serve to postpone the relevance of such a possibility.

Rick's next turn continues the teasing mis-use of verb forms, but
shifts the verb being manipulated from "eat" to "run." He follows
this new error with laughter:

```
515    CARA      (Who) did jou eat at. ₍ehh! •hh
516      RICK                          ⎡But ↑I'm going to go=
517                      ↑I'm gunna go r ran now. °hh-hh-hh°
```

Conjoint production of errors plus shared laughter displays
like-mindedness. By playing along with laughter and more errors,
Cara transforms (at least initially) a potentially antagonistic context – Rick making fun of her – into one in which they share
an orientation towards the talk. They are playing the error game,
together.

Cara could escalate with another form of error, but instead she
repeats his. This displays that she heard him, and it invites him to
confirm, elaborate, or amend what he just said. It does not, however,
escalate the episode with another error, and this possibly moves
towards closing down the laughable-escalation sequence. He repeats
his error, in response to which she laughs:

```
517    RICK      =↑I'm gunna go r- ran now.      °hh-hh-hh°=
518    CARA      =>Y' gonna go< ran?
519    RICK      'm 'nna go ra: ₍n. ⎤
520    CARA                     ⎣nh⎦ ha ↑ha ha ha.=
521    RICK      =•ehh=
```

She then utilizes the mock-insulting "£Fuck you£" retort and a
comic wail (line 527) to display a shift in her orientation to the
laughables: she orients to Rick as laughing *at* her rather than *with*
her:[1]

```
522   CARA    =°£Fuck you.£° ((low, gravelly voice))
523   CARA    ↑•hu:hh. ↑huh-huh huh-huh.
524           (0.4)
525   CARA    °↑Gonna go ra:n  no:wh,  hih-uh-huh-uh°
526   CARA    ↑Huh-huh-huh-huh huh •hh
527   CARA    ↑LEAVE ME AL↑O:NE.
```

Despite Cara's exhortation to "leave her alone," Rick pursues the extended word play with another laughable error, changing the verb from "run" to "go." He follows this with laughter. Cara might laugh here, but instead she repeats his prior turn as a question, changing the error-verb slightly. He repeats the phrase implicitly accepting her amendment to the error term. He laughs within the word "movie," and Cara joins in laughing:[2]

```
527   CARA    [↑LEA' ME AL↑O:NE.]
528   RICK    [N'  'e-    an'    ]then- and ↑then I'm gunnuh-
529   RICK    And then I'm gonna go:un to a movie. °hh hh°
530           (.)
531   CARA    Gonna gone to a movie?
532   RICK    Gonna go:ne to a mov(h)[ie.
533   CARA                           [eh ↑hih hih hn ↑hn hn •hhh
```

So far, both participants have treated Cara's original error as laughable. They subsequently initiated a series of laughables and more laughter. After several escalations, Cara has made a move to discontinue the cluster, but Rick renews with another candidate laughable. The shared laughter reframed the original error as the first of a series, and now the speakers are negotiating how long this cluster of laughables and shared laughs will continue.

The shared laughter that provides sequential basis for the display of conversational play also provides grounds for other interactional business. The error-laughables are not embedded in any random utterances, but specifically in a series of systematically ambiguous turns. On one level they provide talk through which the participants can play with verbs and laugh together, celebrating Cara's error. On another level, however, they hearably continue the possible relevance of going somewhere together. Recall that prior to the original error, Rick had produced a question hearable as pre-invitation (line 498), and Cara's response (line 500) left open the relevancy of an invitation in the next position:

```
498    RICK    Have you had dinner yet?
499            (0.6)
500    CARA    No I haven't. Have you,
```

Subsequent turns seemed to move away from treating the eating talk as pre-invitation. Is Rick's mention now of plans to go see a movie (line 529) also relevant to pre-invitation? Cara orients to this possibility by taking his prior phrase (incorrect verb form and all) and embedding it within a follow-up question. Rick provides a brief, affirmative response:

```
532    RICK    Gonna go:ne to a mov⌐(h)ie.
533    CARA                         ⌊eh ↑hih hih hn ↑hn hn •hhh=
534    CARA    ↑Are you gonna gone to a movie?=
535    RICK    =Yeah.
536            (.)
```

Rick maintains and builds the ongoing ambiguity: (1) word-game; and (2) possible invitation sequence. At line 537, he makes an invitation; but it is done as next in the series of laughables, this one an error-form of the verb "come":

```
534    CARA    ↑Are you gonna gone to a movie?=
535    RICK    =Yeah.
536            (.)
537    RICK    Ya wanna comed?
```

Cara could respond to Rick's turn as an invitation; she could also respond to it as if it were another escalation of the word play. This sequential ambiguity routinely faces recipients of adjacency pair first parts such as questions and invitations:

> Is it serious or is it a joke – or – is he serious or is he joking. For pretty much any such first part-members you can find – either directly on the occurrence of it, or after a response – "You're kidding." "Are you kidding?" "Are you serious?" Now what that utterance is specifically attending is the issue of what sequence that first utterance should generate. . . . "Are you making an offer that I might accept?" – "Or are you joking." (Sacks, 1992, pp. 671–672)

The alternatives being negotiated here might be posed as: is this a "real" invitation? Or is it only a vehicle for more laughables and laughter?

Put in another vocabulary, the issue concerns whether interactants are engaged in *play*. Gregory Bateson (1972, pp. 177–193; see also Goffman, 1974, Chapter 2) characterizes play as an interactional state created by metacommunicative signals which frame or bracket messages as nonserious. Play behavior resembles, but is not the same as, some primary frame of behavior. Thus an animal engaged in play fighting will perform a mock-bite, which denotes, but is not, real combat. Bateson argued that "this phenomenon, play, could only occur if the participant organisms were capable of some degree of metacommunication, *i.e.*, of exchanging signals which would carry the message, 'this is play'" (Bateson, 1972, p. 179).

Framed as play, a conversational act does not carry the "serious" consequences it might otherwise. An impropriety treated as play does not create offense or breach in the interaction. An invitation displayed as play-only makes relevant, not a real answer, but something appreciating the playfulness, such as laughter or a next laughable.

Yet this issue grows more complex in human interaction where sequences can be constructed via metacommunicative signals that display, not "this is play," but "is this play?" (Bateson, 1972, p. 182). Play frames may be ambiguous and are subject to redefinition. The "serious" or playful status of utterances may not be clear to interactants. They may utilize the potential ambiguity inherent in "is this play?" messages to extend an invitation which has not been "really" extended, or perform acceptance which may or may not constitute "real" acceptance. These options provide obvious strategic uses. Both offerer and recipient can test the waters with play-offers and play-acceptances without risking "real" rejection. Should Cara refuse, Rick could retroactively frame his invitation as play only. Should Cara accept, only subsequently to learn that Rick's offer was not real, she could retroactively frame her acceptance as playful. This offers a way to explore ambiguously the possibility of a date. Just as teasing messages are simultaneously play and not-play (Alberts and Hopper, 1982), utterances which are and are not invitations and acceptances may display flirting, courtship, and the like.

So, Cara's displayed interpretation of this turn carries sequential implications – and, of course, relational consequences as well.

Now back to our story. Before Cara can reply to Rick's possibly-playful invitation he gives her more information to go on by laughing and adding the word "no." The negation and laughs mark his invitation as non-serious:

```
537    RICK       Ya wanna comed?
538    RICK       hNo(h)o.
```

Cara treats the invitation as joking. In her reply she embeds a "corrected" version of his verb form. She also maintains the invitation-as-laughable ambiguity: he gave an invitation that may or may not be real, and she gives an acceptance which may or may not be real:

```
537    RICK       Ya wanna comed?
538    RICK       hNo(h)o.
539    CARA       ↑I wanna came.
```

Rick's next utterance displays another shift in the talk. He does not repeat her correction, or even acknowledge it; he does not repeat his prior incorrect grammatical form; and he does not produce a new but also incorrect grammatical form. Rather, his utterance carries hearably *improper* implications:

```
539    CARA       ↑I wanna caɩ me.
540    RICK                   ˡ•ehh ↓Wannih c(h)ome,
```

By employing a "dirty" vocal delivery – a low, husky voice and a within-speech laugh particle – he may invoke in this turn the sexual meaning of "come" as "orgasm." This proposes a different kind of interactional difficulty with which to play: not the relatively innocuous speech errors they have done to this point, but overt sexual innuendo. It is a play within a play within a play, an "is this play?" sexual impropriety (invitation?) embedded within the framework of playful speech errors, which in turn are embedded within talk negotiating ambiguous, possible social invitations.

An impropriety having been introduced, Cara could now participate in building an intimacy display consisting of shared laughter and exchange of improprieties. Yet she treats it as simply another in their series of verb-form distortions, following immediately with her own version shifting the verb from "come" to "came." In effect, she disattends the new, possibly improprietous aspects of this utterance and continues as if it is the more innocuous kind of laughable:

```
540    RICK     •ehh ↓Wannih c(h)⌊ome,
541    CARA                       ⌈↑hnh You wanna came?
```

Various laminations notwithstanding, they share laughter follow-ing this interchange. The shared laughter winds down and there is a pause. Cara repeats her earlier disaffiliative wail (line 547). Ad-ditional brief laugh particles and gaps follow, and the participants seem to have reached a potential winding down of the episode:

```
540    RICK     •ehh ↓Wannih c(h)⌊ome,
541    CARA                       ⌈↑hnh You wanna came?
542    RICK     ⌊•ehhh
543    CARA     ⌊°↑nh nh nh nh hnh hnh°
544             (0.8)
545    CARA     •hhh-hhh
546             (.)
547    CARA     ↑eh heh Leave me a↑lo:::ne!
548    RICK     •ehh
549             (0.7)
550    CARA     ehh
551             (0.2)
```

Cara attempts to extend the episode by introducing a new laughable-error, done as a report of what Leigh Anne said. She laughs at this, and laughter and/or another escalation might now be relevant from Rick. But he remains silent and a noticeable gap follows. Cara forcefully calls on him to laugh (line 557); in response he provides an account (with laughter) for his absence. Cara repeats the laughable from Leigh Anne, inviting affiliation. Rick does not affiliate, but rather questions why he should laugh, and this issue carries their talk forward out of the episode of error-laughables plus shared laughter:

```
552    CARA     °heh° hUhm gonna went home Leigh Anne said.=
553             =eh heh huh ↑hu
554             (0.5)
```

555	CARA	°kh-°hhh
556		(0.2)
557	CARA	↑RI:CK ↑LA:UGH!
558	RICK	I <u>mi</u>ssed it I di(h)dn' hear you(h[°h)]ou°
559	CARA	[She] said
559a		she's gonna we:nt ho:me.
560	RICK	°ehhh WHY DO I HAVE TO L<u>AU</u>GH.
561		(1.0)
562	CARA	↑<u>Cu</u>:z.
563	RICK	Cuz of wh<u>a</u>t. Does it make you <u>fee</u>l better?
564	CARA	It's f<u>u</u>nny. . . .

In summary, a grammatical error provides the starting point for an episode of turns devoted to speech play and mock-errors. Cara repairs the error, displaying initial willingness to proceed without laughter or further notice of it. Rick laughs at the error, and only then does Cara join in laughing. After she produces an additional incorrect verb form as a next laughable, they continue a series of extensions based upon errors in verb tense. Through this word-play both participants maintain potential ambiguity about whether the ongoing talk includes "genuine" social invitations and responses. Rick introduces word-play that also contains an impropriety with sexual overtones. Cara disattends this aspect of his talk while extending the theme of innocuous mock-errors. Rick drops out of the sequence of escalations; a final attempt by Cara to extend the impropriety brings hearable silence from Rick.

Arriving quickly after the occurrence of the error, shared laughter displays participants' willingness to treat the error as laughable. In addition, shared laughter provides a sequentially relevant basis for more of the same: one error having drawn laughs provides warrant for either speaker to produce another error as a means of drawing more laughter. In the context of producing next errors, speakers can provide utterances whose "seriousness" is systematically ambiguous. They can make social invitations, accept those invitations, create sexual innuendo, and more, all relevant as ways to provide for more shared laughter. Thus, shared laughter serves both to process the original error and to pave the way for subsequent displays of play.

It is evident then that laughing along contributes to expanded sequences of teasing and play, providing multiple opportunities for the butt of a tease to play along and for other actions to get accomplished. Through laughter, the butt of the tease or the recipient of the impropriety may find herself caught up in activities that may hurt, offend, or not be wholly welcome. Yet outright resistance can lead one to be considered distant, lacking in humor, stiff, etc. To avoid such labels, one may find it interactionally useful to laugh while also marking some resistance to what is going on. Laughs are ambiguous in how participants may interpret them locally. Through them participants can show appreciation without necessarily affiliating. In fact, as shown in the next section, recipients may, in and through laughter, show (at least partial) *resistance* to the conversational activity in progress.

Resisting

In the preceding pages I have shown how laughing along both accompanies and helps develop trajectories starting with teases and improprieties which may lead to displays of intimacy. I now turn to characterizing ways laughter may contribute to enacting resistance. Structurally, resistance means acting to discontinue the activity proposed or in progress. Victims of teases may reject its substance, and recipients of an impropriety may disattend or disaffiliate from it. Laughter is not necessary to these ways of resisting. Laughter, however, does routinely get implicated in resistance.[3]

Laughing potentially interrupts the flow of an activity, operating metacommunicatively to treat what was said as laughable. In the following example, an aphasic patient laughs while directly rejecting the clinician's instruction:

(In Simmons-Mackie, 2001. Clinician is having trouble understanding what the client is communicating on a therapeutic task.)

> CLINICIAN   Tell me more.
> CLIENT   No (laughs)
> CLINICIAN   Yea, tell me more.

In an instance shown earlier, T complains to S about guns in the possession of members of an urban street gang. S repeats the word "missiles" with laughter.

(CY.SIU.NS.011. TS by N. Stucky)

> T   bl<u>a</u>ck shirts and black pants and (.) sku:ll caps
>   on they face and stuff and they (.) ridin around
>   here sh<u>oo</u>tin' up each other and with techni::nes
>   and I mean missiles automaₜtics-
> S   ⌈mi(h)ssiles ha ha ha

The repetition plus laughter move her away from serious appreciation of the situation T presents; rather, she treats it as overbuilt and
thus teasable. Laughter thus helps the hearer display resistance to
going along "seriously" or unproblematically with this exaggerated
description.

Laughter displays resistance to a proposal. Here, Donna informs
Jack, about thirty seconds into their conversation, that she is recording the phone call. Her appended "Okay?" seeks his agreement. In
response, he laughs and calls on her to account for this decision:

((UTCL A16. TS by B. DeSorbo)

> DONNA   I guess so:=I'm making another tape okay?
>   (0.3)
> JACK   hu huh hh hh=<u>Why</u>:
> DONNA   Cause I really don't want to use that last one.

Laughter can resist troubles-talk. Jefferson (1984) shows how
people engaged in telling about their troubles will laugh. Laughter
in such an environment does not get treated as marking a humorous
laughable but rather as a display on the part of the teller of bravery,
coping, or keeping an appropriate attitude; that is, of resisting the
troubles. Following such moments hearers generally do not laugh,
but take the talk seriously, thereby showing a sympathetic stance
towards the troubles-teller. Here, Emma describes physical symptoms, punctuated within-speech and post-utterance with laugh particles. Lottie does not laugh along, but offers an explanation for the
symptoms.

(NB:IV:4:4:SO, in Jefferson, 1984, p. 347)

> E   You ought to see me broken out to<u>day</u> God I
>   t(hh)ook a ba:th, and I'm just a ma:ss of b-
>   little p(h)imp(h)les:: heh heh ⌈•hhh
> L   ⌈Oh <u>that's</u> from
>   uh:: n-nerves.

Despite this regular pattern (troubles-teller laughs, recipient does not), two alternative patterns may be found. In some instances, recipients will laugh along during what Jefferson (p. 351) calls a "buffer topic." This is when troubles teller introduces some light-hearted materials in the environment of troubles telling. Laughing along at such moments is oriented not to the troubles themselves but to the humorous aside. There are also exceptional cases in which the recipient of troubles-telling laughs. Jefferson argues that such recipient laughter marks resistance to the troubles. At A's complaint "*I'm sick* abou:t it" M produces a particle of laughter (see first arrow). A's report that she sometimes breaks into tears elicits serious response. Then the display of regret draws lengthy laughter (second arrow below).

(SBL:IV:6:16-20:SO:S, in Jefferson, 1984, pp. 365–366. A is lamenting about having gotten rid of a family cat.)

	A	I: <u>still</u> feel that I did the <u>wr</u>ong thing. And <u>I'm</u> <u>sick</u> abou:t it,
→	M	₁₁<u>ehhh</u>
	A	⁽⁽<u>Sometimes</u> I feel so (0.4) ( ) I <u>really</u> feel (0.2) <u>so</u> tired and sort of (0.3) a<u>lone</u> and everything I can go into <u>tears</u> about it no (0.2)
	A	<u>n</u>₁o <u>kidd</u>₁ing I feel real <u>badly</u> abo₁ ut it
	M	⁺hh ⁺Yeh w e l l <u>that's</u> <u>tru-</u>⁾
	M	Ah hah you <u>really</u> <u>do</u>₁ miss ( ).
	A	⁺He was in our <u>house</u> a <u>little</u> friend and I gave him aw<u>a</u>:y.
→	M	Yeh- uhh <u>hahh</u> hahh₁ hu- •uhhh
	A	⁺And I feel <u>SO</u> <u>badly</u> about it Simply aw::ful.

The troubles-teller A pitifully laments that she "gave away" a "little friend." M laughs, displaying resistance to aligning with this (seemingly escalating) reporting of troubles.

As these examples show, laughter plays a part in resisting topical development, the sequential import of a first pair part, or complaining talk. Yet laughter may also go along with the activity. There is a third possibility between these two, which involves minimally laughing along in a way which, at the same time, resists. In the example shown in the next section, the butt of a sexual tease laughs along while marking resistance.

Case study: "Even wilder"

The following instance comes from the radio program "Car Talk," broadcast live on National Public Radio affiliate stations. In the show, brothers Tom and Ray Magliozzi, who run an automobile repair shop in the Boston area, dispense advice to people calling in with car-related problems. In addition to giving advice, the brothers joke and play, often punctuating the talk with laughter. The show combines face-to-face interaction between Tom and Ray, telephone interaction with the caller, and broadcasting to an overhearing radio audience. The interactions with callers typically reflect a structure common to other advice-based talk shows: opening, problem for- mulating, advising, and closing (Crow, 1986).

The fragment under consideration is shown in its entirety below. It comes from the beginning of a phone call, the second one broad- cast on this particular day:

("Car Talk," National Public Radio, 30 March 1997 Tom and Ray Magliozzi and Caller; transcribed by T. Arduini, P. Glenn)

```
1     RAY      One eight hundred (.) three three two (.)
2              nine two eight seven=Hello you're on Car
3              Talk.
4     CHAND    ↑Hi, this is Chandler?, I'm calling from
5              Denver?
6     RAY      ↑Chandler=
7     TOM      =↑Sh⌊::andler
8     CHAND         ⌈Yes
9     RAY      From ↑Denver=
10    CHAND    =Yes
11    TOM      ↑Sh:andler
12    RAY      Th⌊at's an unusual (.) first name?
13    CHAND       ⌈Yes
14    CHAND    Well (.) I kno⌊w I'm not supposed to tell you-
15    RAY                    ⌈for- for a woman
16    CHAND    my last name my last name's even wilder.
17             (0.9)
```

18	CHAND	=ₗAnyway
19	TOM	=ˡ↑Even wi̲lder
20	CHAND	Yes=
21	TOM	=Ooh! Chandler's even wilder than the la̲st
22		girlₗ I went out with
23	RAY	ˡHu hu hu ha haₗ ha ha ha ha
24	CHAND	ˡH̲hhₗh hhh huh huh huh huhₗ
25	TOM	ˡHAH HAH HAH HAH HAHˡ=
26	TOM	ₗHAH HAH HAH HAH HAH (.) •hhₗ huh huh
27	CHAND	=ˡhuh huh •u h h h h ˡW↑e:ll.
28	RAY	ˡThere's a-
29		there's a hyphen in there?
30	CHAND	ehNo
31	TOM	No it's just a sentence
32	CHAND	It's just aₗ sentence? That's right
33	TOM	ˡHa ha ha ha ha ha ha ha •hh •hh
34	RAY	°Well?°
35	CHAND	Anyway, ↑I̲: have (.) I have this problem. I
36		have a Ford Escort (.) wagon (.)

Of particular interest for this chapter are lines 21–27. In lines 21–22, Tom playfully assesses the caller as "even wilder" in contrast to "the last girl" he went out with. In this utterance he treats the caller as female, as someone he might go out with, and as "wild" with sexual implications (I will develop these claims below). All three participants laugh, although her laughter displays a less affiliative stance towards the laughable than those of the brothers. Through features of her laughter, Chandler manages both to *laugh along* with the sexual jest and to *resist* it.

Tom's jest (lines 21–22) becomes understandable by tracing how from the opening moments of the interaction the caller's name gets topicalized and serves as a resource for playfulness. She initially identifies herself as "Chandler from Denver." This use of first-name-only plus location for self-identification is standard practice on the show.[4]

| 4 | CHAND | ↑Hi, this is Chandler?, I'm calling from |
| 5 | | Denver? |

Her name gets immediate and marked attention. Ray repeats it with increased melody and emphasis; Tom does the same, shifting the pronunciation of the initial affricate <u>ch</u> to <u>sh</u> and stretching it.

4	CHAND	↑Hi, this is Chandler?, I'm calling from
5		Denver?
6	RAY	↑<u>Chandler</u>=
7	TOM	=↑<u>Sh</u>⌐::and<u>l</u>er
8	CHAND	⌐Yes

Repeats can function as next-turn repair initiators (Schegloff, Jefferson, and Sacks, 1977). At the least, they retrieve some prior item and make it available for further talk or action. (They also divert participants, at least momentarily, from moving towards the purpose of the call; in "Car Talk" such playful diversions are common.) Consistent with the structure of repair sequences, the repeat returns the floor to the other to confirm or amend the repeated item. In overlap with Tom's second repeat, Chandler confirms that this is her name.

Ray now repeats the second half of Chandler's self-identification, "from Denver". This repeat has a marked melody paralleling that which he used in repeating her name a moment earlier. It is a poetic moment: the melody echo emphasizes the repeated last phoneme of "Chandler" and "Denver". This too fitting the structure of a next-turn repair initiator, it returns the floor to her, and she confirms "Denver" as correct.

7	TOM	=↑<u>Sh</u>⌐::and<u>l</u>er
8	CHAND	⌐Yes
9	RAY	From ↑Denver=
10	CHAND	=Yes

Tom repeats the name again (line 11), once more with marked, melodic intonation. She again confirms it.

11	TOM	↑Sh:andler
13	CHAND	Yes

That it's been repeated multiple times, and already confirmed, provides evidence that this is not a problem of hearing or understanding on their part. Rather, the repetitions open up possibilities

for topicalizing her name as something to talk about, and/or keying a playful treatment of it (on repetition's role in keying play, see
Hopper and Glenn, 1994).

Ray assesses the name as "unusual" (line 12) and thus contributes
further to the caller's name becoming topicalized. Chandler responds
by stating that she knows the show's rule about callers not providing
last name and then assesses her last name as "even wilder":

```
11    TOM      ↑Sh:andler
12    RAY      Tha⌐t's an unusual (.) first name?
13    CHAND        ⌐Yes
14    CHAND    Well (.) I kno⌐w I'm not supposed to tell you-
16             my last name my last name's even wilder.
```

The comparative form "even wilder" implicitly assesses the name
"Chandler" as "wild." Arguably, "wild" represents an upgrade in
assessment intensity from Ray's preceding use of "unusual." To this
point, then, the three interactants have given her name marked treatment through repetition, playful intonation, and assessments.

In overlap with Chandler's turn, Ray (line 15) produces a delayed
completion (Lerner, 1989) of his prior turn (line 12):

```
12    RAY      Tha⌐t's an unusual (.) first name?
14    CHAND    Well (.) I kno⌐w I'm not supposed to tell you-
15    RAY              ⌐for- for a woman
16    CHAND    my last name my last name's even wilder.
```

This added prepositional phrase modifies his assessment such that
the name "Chandler" is unusual, not for all people, but "for a
woman." Her unfolding turn, which shifts focus from her first name
to her (unstated) last name, does not attend explicitly to the delayed
completion. After she says her last name is "even wilder," there
is a pause. Several possibilities are relevant here. They could talk
more about her first name; they could talk about her wild but unstated last name; they could go on with the business of the call.
Chandler speaks next, saying "Anyway" as a way to mark willingness to close this section of talk and move on. In overlap, Tom
repeats her preceding phrase "even wilder." She confirms his repeat. He produces a joke, prefaced by an exclamation of delight or
excitement:

16 CHAND   my last name my last name's even wilder.
17   (0.9)
18 CHAND   =⌊Anyway
19 TOM   =⌈↑Even wilder
20 CHAND   Yes=
21 TOM   =Ooh! Chandler's even wilder than the last
22   girl I went out with

Considering the basis for this joke provides insight into the gendering of this talk. He repeats the assessment "even wilder" but applies
it to her, not to her last name, as she had previously done. To retain
the contrastive form of the adverb–adjective assessing pair (which is
necessary for the word play), Tom must provide something or someone against which to compare Chandler. He does so by inventing
"the last girl" he went out with. In this clever jibe he uses her words
to assess her by invoking a non-existent dating/romantic relationship between them and implying that within it she is wild (with a
possibly sexual meaning).

Now comes the laughter. Ray begins to laugh immediately after
the words "last girl," displaying recognition of the joke in progress.
His is an open-mouthed cackle, lengthy and mirthful.

21 TOM   =Ooh! Chandler's even wilder than the last
22   girl ⌊I went out with
23 RAY   ⌈Hu hu hu ha ha ha ha ha ha

Chandler starts laughing at completion of Tom's utterance and following several syllables of Ray's laugh. She produces two initial
closed-mouth syllables (the first with emphasis), six open-mouth
syllables, and an audible inbreath. Tom's is the biggest laugh of all,
loud and hearty (lines 25–26). It comes immediately upon completion of his laughable, and following onset of Ray's and Chandler's
laughs. It is consistent with the "other speaker laughs first" rule
discussed in Chapter 3.

21 TOM   =Oooh! Chandler's even wilder than the last
22   girl⌊ I went out with
23 RAY   ⌈Hu hu hu ha ha⌊ ha ha ha ha
24 CHAND   ⌈Hhₗhh hhh huh huh huh hⱼuh
25 TOM   ⌈HAH HAH HAH HAH HAH⌋=

26   TOM   ₍HAH HAH HAH HAH HAH (.)   •hh huh huh
27   CHAND   =ˡhuh huh •u h h h h

This spate of shared laughter soon shows signs of winding down.
Ray's laugh stream ceases (line 23), Chandler produces an audible
inbreath (line 27), and Tom pauses briefly and produces an audible
inbreath (line 26). Tom follows the inbreath with two additional
laugh particles which (as discussed in Chapter 4) may show willingness to keep laughing and may constitute an invitation to renew
and extend shared laughter. At that moment, however, Chandler
resumes non-laughing talk, and Tom ceases laughing.

26   TOM   ₍HAH HAH HAH HAH HAH (.)   •hh₍ huh huh
27   CHAND   =ˡhuh huh •u h h h h   ˡW↑e:ll.

Recall that talking on topic represents a standard option for moving
out of shared laughter. Chandler's response "W↑e:ll" discontinues
laughter, displays resistance to the previous talk, yet maintains a
tone of playfulness. "Well" does not in and of itself offer talk on
topic. It can mark and precede disagreement or resistance. In the
following example, Emma asks daughter Barbara to call her father
(Emma's husband; apparently he and Emma have argued, and he has
gone away). Barbara's resistance is evident in the pause following
the request, in the weak agreement particle "yeah," and the coun-
terproposal that follows "well." It appears evident to Emma too,
for she persists with an offer that implies Barbara calling her father.
Barbara again resists, marked at the outset by "well," and now directly provides a reason for not calling her father: she does not wish
to "get involved."

(NB:IV:7:R:4. TS by G. Jefferson.)

     EMMA   EN B<u>A</u>RBRA <u>wou</u>ldju <u>CA</u>:LL im dihni̱:ght f<u>o</u>r me, h
             (.)
     BARB   Ye:ah,
     EMMA   •h HU:<u>H</u>?h
     BARB   Well if ↑<u>he</u> dezn't <u>co</u>:me I won't u<u>h</u>:: (0.2) t-
             dra:g (.) <u>Hugh</u> en ↓everybuddy d<u>o</u>:wn↓
     EMMA   CUZ <u>I</u>:'<u>D</u> L::<u>OVE</u> duh (.) <u>cook</u> for yuh,
     BARB   W<u>e</u>:ll I don't- <u>you</u> know I don'wanna git'nv<u>o</u>:lved
             ((talk continues))

"Well" operates as a component of the dispreferred turn shape (see Pomerantz, 1984, pp. 63–64) that marks second pair parts which display resistance, such as disagreeing with an opinion, minimizing a compliment, refusing an offer, or denying a request.

Chandler utters "W↑e:ll." with elongation and upward intonation[5] that suggests something like mock indignation. Placed here, following Tom's jest about her "wildness" plus shared laughter, it expresses resistance (albeit playful) to what has just gone on. Further evidence for this appears in what happens next. Ray immediately moves the talk away from the laughable plus shared laughter to resume speaking. His reference to "hyphen" via an implicit pun invites a hearing that "even wilder" literally is her last name, i.e., "Chandler Even-Wilder."

| 27 | CHAND | ⌐W↑e:ll. |
| 28–9 | RAY | ⌐There's a- there's a hyphen in there? |

This grammatical jest provides a way for them to continue playing with the caller's name without continuing the more flirtatious, sexual talk. Tom laughs, but neither of the other participants does. Chandler then moves on to the business of the call:

28–9	RAY	There's a- there's a hyphen in there?
30	CHAND	ehNo
31	TOM	No it's just a sentence
32	CHAND	It's just a⌐sentence? That's right
33	TOM	⌐Ha ha ha ha ha ha ha ha •hh •hh
34	RAY	°Well?°
35	CHAND	Anyway, ↑I: have (.) I have this problem. I
36		have a Ford Escort (.) wagon (.)

In this passage, Tom uses Chandler's name and her own words to construct a sexual jest about her. The brothers' laughs align with each other and appreciate the jest that is done (however innocuously) at her expense. By laughing at the sexual jest, Chandler displays some willingness to play along. By moving first to terminate shared laughter and registering objection with the playfully indignant "Well" she displays some resistance to the jest. By resuming talk she helps move them away from the sexual reference. At the first sign of lack of enthusiasm from Chandler, they immediately move away from sexual innuendo, and they continue talking about matters for which sex seems not to be foregrounded: a hyphen in the hyphenated last name and the problem about which she called the show.[6]

In summary, Chandler uses laughter to both play along and show resistance. She joins in shared laughter, ceases laughing, and produces the lexical item "W↑e:ll." which playfully distances her from the preceding (sexual) jibes. Sensitive to this, Ray immediately shifts talk so that playfulness continues but sexual innuendo does not. Features of the interactional workings of laughter make Chandler's response possible. Laughter alone ambiguously affiliates with its referent. It may accompany either outright rejection, overt affiliation and escalation, or a mid-range position of appreciation with resistance. This middle course may be understood as the kind of laughter people produce when faced with a situation demanding politeness yet provoking discomfort.

Coda: on gender and laughter

When I first heard this instance, I felt that Tom and Ray's teasing of Chandler was distinctly gendered. As I studied it more, I felt certain that she was responding through her laughter in a way that women often do to sexual teases from men. Is this a gendered moment? What evidence might there be for making an empirical case for participant orientation to gender in laughter?

Previous chapters have shown that shared laughter commonly begins by one person laughing first to invite another to laugh along. Commonly, however, other speakers choose not to accept laugh invitations. What regularities in the sequential organization of talk underlie these possibilities of laughing along or not? What kinds of interactional work get done, what sort of situational relevancies displayed? One possibility, suggested both in scholarly and popular sources, is that women are more likely to laugh than are men. Is gender relevant to the organization of who laughs with whom? The examples below illustrate this possibility.

(UTCL A10HAMLE.14:5-6. TS by R. Hopper.)

| 162 | RICK | Ye::ah I oh I called up- immediately after |
| 163 | | work= |

```
164   RICK    =I said <<what the fuck>> Billy man:
165→  RICK    You're pissin' me o(h)(h)ff=
166→  JES     =ehhh huh °hh°=
167   RICK    =>>An he goes<< (0.2) Whattaya g' |do
168           just rag on me?
```

In telling a story to Jes, Rick reports what he had said to another person. In the final word of this utterance, "off," he embeds two laugh particles. Immediately following this, Jes laughs. Rick then continues his telling. The male laughs first at his own laughable, and the female laughs along.

In the following instance, however, the female laughs first at her own laughable, but the male does not laugh along:

(UTCL A10BROWN.2:7. TS by R. Hopper.)

```
196   JOY     pt •hhh Well call us here on Sunday
197           ((noise))
198           (0.4)
199   JOY     And- (0.2) uwhat's that
200   SKEET   Are you there?
201   JOY     Yeah
202           (0.4)
203   SKEET   Yeah go ahead
204   JOY     And u:m let us know whether you can (0.4)
205           take all of us to m(h)ovie or n(h)ot(h)
206           hih hih
207   SKEET   (Uk) I will do that
208           (0.2)
209   SKEET   I will do that
```

Joy playfully instructs Skeet to call so that he can treat her and several friends to a movie. She laughs within and following completion of this turn at talk (lines 205–206). Skeet agrees to call her. He does not, however, laugh with her.

A common assumption of much sociolinguistic and communication research is that particular features of speech or interaction reflect and constitute sex differences. There are claims that women use more tag questions, disclaimers, and hedges, and that men interrupt women more than women do men. Tannen (1990) asserts that women give more audible and visible feedback when listening than men do. Wood (1996, p. 157) summarizes research findings indicating a tendency for women to do more "conversational maintenance" work, including behaviors to signal interest and involvement. A consistent finding across psychological studies is that women smile more than men (LaFrance and Hecht, 1999, p. 50).

Researchers offer various conceptual explanations for such differences. Some argue that these may not reflect actual behavioral differences as much as the fact that people perceive women and men as speaking differently (Hopper, 2002). Initially researchers were willing to explain such differences in terms of lesser confidence or competence on the part of women. Recent studies tend to treat such claims as problematic (see West, 1995), and suggest that differences may in fact show women as being highly competent, perhaps more so than men. Another explanation is that speech features reflect varying degrees of relative power or status, and that when these variables are controlled, many of the gender differences no longer appear significant (LaFrance and Hecht, 1999, p. 50). Others account for variations as reflecting different primary styles of communication. Pushed to an extreme, style-difference arguments pose women and men as coming from different cultures (Tannen, 1990) or even different planets (Gray, 1992).

Laughter may be one feature of discourse through which people display and constitute gender differences. Some gender stereotypes and research support this possibility. Adams and Kirkevold (1977) observed laughter in fast-food restaurants and concluded that in general females laughed more than males, and that females 12–17 years of age laughed more than people of any other particular age–sex grouping. There are shared cultural assumptions (perhaps based in stereotypes) that men produce more laughable, humorous behavior, and that women do more laughing in response to men, than the converse. Indeed, Adelsward (1989) found such a trend in her data drawn from a variety of casual and institutional interactions in Sweden. Laughter can display involvement or interest and help with relationship or interaction "maintenance." If women more commonly handle such interactional chores, then it might also be that women do more laughing in the presence of, and responsive to, men than vice versa. In an observational study, Provine (2000, p. 28) found that in dyadic interactions, females are more likely to laugh along when males produce laughables than males are when

Table 6.1 *Distribution of laughs by sex and by shared/not shared*

	First laugh by	No second laugh	Second by other
Female	30	23	7
Male	33	20	13

(From Jefferson, 1994)

females produce laughable utterances. Pollio and Edgerly (1976, p. 240) conclude from analysis of social settings that "most laughter is initiated by men and that women much more frequently laugh or smile, but hardly ever joke, in these contexts." Does close analysis of transcribed, recorded, naturalistic interaction bear out these patterns?

Investigating gender–laughter differences in naturalistic interaction presents intriguing challenges and, so far, ephemeral results. Jefferson (1994) explored the possibility, common in popular belief, that "In male–female interaction, if the male laughed, the female would join in laughing; if the female laughed, the male would not join in laughing" (p. 1). She conducted a preliminary count of instances drawn from various recorded, transcribed, two-party conversations between a female and a male, in which laughter occurred. Out of 63 total instances of laughter, 20 received a second laugh from the co-participant, while 43 did not. Females initiated 23 of the 43 instances of unshared laughter, compared to the males' 20. Females initiated 7 of 20 instances of shared laughter, compared to the males' 13. Table 6.1 summarizes these numbers.

Although there seems to be a slight trend in the predicted direction, it is too slight, and the sample size too small, to make any claim of significance. The simple count failing to bear out a claim of gender difference, Jefferson then turned to a more complex, case-by-case analysis of sequential activities within which laughter occurs, to see if there might be some other basis for people *perceiving* a gender–laughter distinction. When she grouped instances by whether laughing along or not would display receptiveness or resistance to the activity of the first laugher, she found a tentative pattern. It is this: males tend to exhibit what Jefferson calls "laugh-resistance";

that is, when it's clear that laughter has been invited, they will more likely refuse to laugh along. However, if first laugh is not inviting shared laughter but accompanying troubles-telling, then not-laughing displays troubles-receptiveness (Jefferson, 1984). In such cases, males are more likely to laugh along, but the laughing now displays resistance to receiving troubles-talk. Females, Jefferson argued, showed the reverse pattern. When first laugh by male is inviting laughter, they will tend to provide second laugh. When first laugh by male speaker shows resistance to his own troubles, female will affiliate by not laughing along. Emphasizing the gross caricatures implied by these simple binary categories, she refers to the actors as "Tarzan" and "Jane" in summarizing the pattern as follows:

Tarzans interacting with Janes exhibit "laugh-resistance" except when exhibiting "laugh-resistance" would itself constitute a display of "troubles-receptiveness," in which case Tarzans exhibit "laugh-receptiveness" and, thereby, exhibit "troubles-resistance."

Likewise, we can propose that Janes interacting with Tarzans exhibit "laugh-receptiveness" except when exhibiting "laugh-receptiveness" would itself constitute a display of "troubles-resistance," in which case Janes exhibit "laugh-resistance" and, thereby, exhibit "troubles-receptiveness." (pp. 15–16)

The most fundamental summary of these claims is that "Janes interacting with Tarzans exhibit receptiveness and Tarzans interacting with Janes exhibit resistance" (p. 17). In other words, the regular usage of laughter is altered to display regularities in a higher-order activity type of troubles-telling – "higher order" in that uses of laughter to display orientation to troubles-telling seem to take precedence over showing laugh resistance or receptiveness. Both laughter and troubles-telling may be understood as subordinate to a more fundamental activity, displaying receptiveness–resistance.

Jefferson is careful to mark these claims as tentative. She does not return to count instances according to the trends identified in the case-by-case analysis. She also suggests that the trends may be more perceptual than actual. This is consistent with the claims of some gender scholars that communicative sex differences are less about actual behavior and more about people's socialized patterns of perceiving how women and men communicate.

Table 6.2 *Distribution of laughs by sex and by shared/not shared*

	First laugh by	No second laugh	Second by other
Female	101	74	27
Male	70	44	26

(From Glenn, Hoffman, and Hopper, March 1996)

We set out in a research project (Glenn, Hoffman, and Hopper, 1996) to test Jefferson's "caricatures" among additional instances of female–male two-party interaction. We selected talk of people whose relationship is at least superficially characterizable as acquaintance, friend, courtship relevant, or romantic-intimate (excluding female–male interactions characterizable as strangers, co-workers, family members, etc.). Using these criteria, we selected a data set of twelve separate female–male two-party interactions, varying in length from one to approximately sixty minutes. For each possible occurrence of laughter found within the corpus of interactions, we coded who (female or male) produced the laughable, who produced the first laugh, whether a second laugh was relevant, whether a second laugh occurred, and if so, by whom. After some more refining of categories and reliability checks, we created a sample of 171 instances for analysis (see Table 6.2).

A simple counting did not reveal substantive sex differences. In 70 instances of male laughing first, 26 times female laughed along (37%). In 101 instances of female laughing first, male joined in 27 times (27%). This does reflect a difference in the hypothesized direction (females laughing along with males more often than the converse), but not a statistically significant one ($X^2 = 2.10$, 1 df).

While examining individual instances, we began to suspect that the type of relationship interaction was making some difference. We distinguished between two broad categories. "Courtship relevant" interactions occur between people whose relationships seem to involve romance, intimacy, flirtation, or friendship tinged with courtship possibilities. In a second group of "other" interactions (mostly acquaintances or friends) interactants do not foreground this relevancy of courtship. We also separated by kind of laughable, distinguishing those for which second laugh is relevant and affiliative (following a humorous, playful laughable) from those for which it is not (self-deprecation, tease, inadvertent error, etc.). When we began to separate types of interactions in this way, we observed some differences. No claims permit tests of significance or safe generalizations due to small cell size resulting from so many categories. Nevertheless, they suggest some possibilities. Specifically, we found that:

1. Outside of courtship-relevant interactions, when a current speaker produced laughable plus first laugh, males responded more to females' laugh invitations than females to males'.
2. Within courtship-relevant interactions, when a current speaker of a funny or playful laughable did not laugh first, but the recipient laughed first, males infrequently ratified their interlocutor's first laugh, while females always did.
3. Laughs for which a second laugh is not relevant (troubles-telling, self-deprecation, tease of other) are relatively much more common in courtship than outside of it, are more often at females' expense than at males', and are more often done by females than by males.

In summary, coding and cross-tabulating yield evidence suggesting that gender may bear some relevance to the organization of laughter, at least for participants in courtship-relevant interactions. To extend the study along these lines would require increasing sample size, including a wider variety of ages and relationships, and seeking more sophisticated ways to characterize different interactional environments.

This search for sex differences in conversational laughter, however intriguing, presents conceptual and methodological problems. Coding necessitates treating the complexities of human interaction as though they could be neatly divided into binary categories such as female/male, laughs/does not laugh, or courtship-relevant/non-courtship-relevant interaction. Even when categories are not binary but allow for more possibilities, the simple act of categorization obscures the situated, in-the-moment production of identity, behavior, relationship, and so forth. Coding, as a method, requires eliminating ambiguity. When it is unclear whether an instance is an example of X or Y, a decision must be made or the instance cannot be used. Yet the very ambiguity of interactional situations provides resources people use in creating and interpreting messages. Although coding allows some first glimpse into differential distributions of interactional phenomena based on gender, detailed examination of actual instances remains the ultimate proving ground for any claims about the relevance of gender to laughter.

In studies such as the ones summarized above, researchers claiming (or seeking) evidence of gender differences notice trends across numbers of cases. Conclusions often reflect this in pro-quantifier terms like "more often" or "less likely." It may be that researchers conclude, at some point, that women are "more likely" to laugh along with men and that men "more often" do not laugh along with women when they might. However, we do not live our communicative lives in the aggregate. We live them one moment at a time, or, in researcher's terms, one instance at a time. If people communicate differently from each other, and if they do so systematically in some way linked to biological sex or gender role, then our task as analysts is to examine the means by which people accomplish such differences in single instances.

Increasingly, scholars are calling for more context-sensitive treatments of gender as socially constituted (see Wodak, 1997, p. 2). Gender is an omnirelevant variable (Garfinkel, 1967, p. 118) in that humans continually display features readable as gendered. However, this does not mean that as participants in interaction we *orient to* gender equally at all times. Many individual attributes or features of context are potentially available as participant resources in the ongoing tasks of organizing and making sense of conduct. Likewise, gender is but one of many features analysts may draw on when explaining communicative phenomena. How can we develop and support a grounded claim for gendered communication being part of a particular communicative moment?

This is but one example of the larger issue of tracing connections between text and context (see Tracy, 1998). An ethnomethodological, CA approach treats context as emergent, fluid, and locally occasioned by participants in interaction. From such a perspective (one advocated by Schegloff [1992] among others), we may make the strongest empirical claims about the relevance of some feature of context (such as gender) in explaining communicative phenomena when evidence exists in the data that participants themselves orient to that feature as relevant. This "intrinsic-to-messages" approach (Hopper, 1992) helps avoid the danger of the researcher imposing a priori theories which may unduly limit or mislead analysis. That is, context-insensitive research risks committing a Type 1 error, claiming the significant relevance of gender when such relevance actually is an artifact of the research and not a part of the realities of the people being studied. This argument leads us away from searching for gender differences and towards a more fundamental search for evidence of participant orientation to gender.

The "Car Talk" instance analyzed above provides evidence that people may orient to gender in the organization of conversational laughter. Ray first explicitly genders the scene by assessing Chandler's name as unusual "for a woman":

```
12   RAY      Th[at's an unusual (.) first name?
14   CHAND    Well (.) I kno[w I'm not supposed to tell you-
15   RAY                     [for- for a woman
```

Moments later, Tom makes the humorous remark at which they all laugh:

```
21   TOM      =Ooh! Chandler's even wilder than the last
22            girl[ I went out with
23   RAY          [Hu hu hu ha ha[   ha ha ha ha
24   CHAND                        [Hhh[h hhh huh huh huh  huh]
25   TOM                              [HAH HAH HAH HAH HAH]=
26   TOM      [HAH HAH    HAH HAH HAH (.) •hh[ huh huh
27   CHAND    =[huh huh •u h h h h              [W↑e:ll.
28   RAY                                        [There's a-
29            there's a hyphen in there?
```

Ray and Tom both place Chandler in the same binary gender category, but they use different terms, "woman" and "girl." Tom's use of "girl" in the jest about her being "even wilder" suggests a younger orientation and perhaps playfulness on his part. It seems fitted as category to the activity "go out with" (See Sacks, 1992, on category bound activities). More specific than simply the broad categories "female" and "male," the talk now invokes, albeit jokingly, participant identities as heterosexual female and male who represent, for each other, potentially dateable (sexual) partners. For such persons, the assessments "wild" or "even wilder" may carry sexual meanings. In this instance, it is not just *gender* which creeps into talk (Hopper and LeBaron, 1998); it is also *sex* – the act, not the biological category.

As the more detailed analysis earlier in this chapter shows, Chandler both laughs along and resists. She moves to close down shared laughter by an inbreath and the word "Well" uttered with a playfully offended tone. In this she orients to the sexual nature of the moment. Evidence that Ray treats her response this way lies in his moving immediately to a non-sexual, perhaps even non-gendered next jest. So: they orient to sex and gender in both laughable and laughter. Furthermore, this pattern is thought to be a common one in female–male interaction: the male makes a sexual, flirtatious, or teasing comment; the female laughs along; if the female does not fully co-implicate in the remark, she will resist only in an indirect, subtle way.

Participants mark the relevance of sex categories and sexuality as features of context. They do so in the service of word-play and shared laughter. *The laughs themselves reflect and constitute different orientations to this invoking of context.* Laughs orient to context through their acoustic features, length, and sequential placement, all of which contribute to marking laughter's footing in relation to the laughable, the participants, and the situation. The instance here turns out to be consistent with Jefferson's preliminary claim that, in laughing along, "Janes interacting with Tarzans exhibit receptiveness" (Jefferson, 1994, p. 17); that is, her laughing shows her to be receptive to what the brothers are about. This "Jane" may not be thrilled about what happens, but she is willing to laugh along while at the same time – through features of her laughter – distancing herself somewhat from the stance of the two Tarzans.

The choice to laugh or not to laugh provides partial clues for hearers and analysts concerning the "work" that laughter may be doing. Placement and production features of laughs further guide our interpretations. Although explication remains challenging, it does seem possible to account empirically for the relevance of gender – and thus, context – to the sequential organization of laughter in interaction. The laughing that women and men do may not always differ from each other, but laughter stands as one of a host of phenomena through which we engender sexual identities.

7

Closing remarks

In this chapter I wish to summarize major themes, discuss some implications, and make bridges to related research agendas. As shown in the first chapter, laughter has long held fascination for those contemplating its nature, causes, functions, and meanings. Biological and ethological researchers demonstrate its close association with related primate behaviors and offer compelling theories of its origins in human communication and its evolutionary functions. The universality of laughter suggests a trans-situational, trans-cultural set of forms and meanings. It is universal that people produce laughter from the same finite set of phonemes and combinations thereof. It is universal that laughter connects to a finite set of facial expressions, breathing rhythms, and body movements. Laughter seems universally associated with feeling enjoyment, perceiving something as funny, or triumphing at other's misfortunes. However, this is not to say that all laughs appear the same, mean the same, or do the same work. Within these general parameters exists considerable latitude for variation in sound, sight, and feeling. As with all forms of human communicative behavior, laughter does far more than stand simply as outer display in any kind of pure mood–sign relation. It may be feigned; it may be done in order to experience certain feelings as well as occurring as a result of those feelings. Notions like "nervous" or "polite" laughter point to its doing other interactional work than simply expressing emotion. Shifting from treating laughter as behavior to treating it as communication opens up consideration of these factors plus others such as how it is offered, placed, accepted, rejected, treated, and shared. Such a shift also allows investigation into cultural and contextual variation.

Philosophers and social scientists have attempted to explain laughter as provoked by humor, exploring various theories for what makes us laugh (i.e., what makes something funny). Attempts to come up with a grand theory for laughter and humor encounter its elusive nature. Feelings of superiority, incongruity, and relief each work at times to make us laugh; none is always present. The "pleasant psychological shift" theory (Morreall, 1983) attractively incorporates elements of the other three. However, it remains rooted in a conception of laughter as the outward expression of an inner state prompted by some stimulus. Laughter may indeed be this, but it is not necessarily so. More recently, researchers across the social sciences have explored more complex explanatory models including physiological, psychological, and social variables that influence human laughter. Physical processes accompanying laughter are more thoroughly known and understood than ever before. The evidence continues to mount that hearty laughter produces positive physical and mental effects. More broadly, it is now widely accepted that a positive, humorous outlook on life (which is both reflected in and supported by laughter) contributes to individual health and well-being. These conclusions have fueled more research into humor and laughter as physical and psychological processes. Here is a case where, for once, something appears both very enjoyable and good for us.

Approaches that explain laughing solely as individual behavior neglect its essentially interactional nature. Whether one laughs, at what, when, how, and for how long, are all influenced by social factors. People seem more likely to laugh when others are present and laughing than when alone or in the presence of others not laughing. People also seem more likely to perceive stimuli as humorous under the same circumstances. However, studies yielding such results have tended to rely on artificial, controlled settings sacrificing naturalistic contexts for the sake of experimental control. They also have emphasized passive viewing of film or video, thus creating situations more closely resembling being in an audience than interpersonal interaction. Despite a wealth of philosophical, theoretical, and scientific attention, we have until recently lacked accounts of laughter's communicative workings in human interaction.

Chapter 2 introduces CA as a research method well suited to producing grounded, emic descriptions and interpretations of how people organize and produce talk-in-interaction. Steeped in the eth-nomethodological tradition developed by Garfinkel and Sacks, CA studies have yielded a wealth of findings based on analysis of recordings of naturalistic interactions. Previous CA research on laughter demonstrates that laughter is finely ordered in its sequential placement and interactional workings. The smallest particles of laughter are shown to be orderly. Laughs coordinate finely with breathing, speech, and other activities. The ability to study recordings and transcripts repeatedly allows us to gain access to this subtle yet powerful precision. From these initial descriptions of micro-level details, successive chapters move to more macro-level observations about sequential environments within which laughs occur and to which they contribute.

Chapter 3 focuses on shared laughter and shows the ways through which people begin and extend it. Gail Jefferson first noticed that people rarely begin laughing together simultaneously; rather, most shared laughs begin with a first invitation and a second laughing along. Chapter 3 furthers these findings in various ways. One involves exploration of visual features of shared laughter. A case study shows how a laugh invitation is issued after recipient shows willingness to laugh by smiling and gazing. Thus, for face-to-face interactions, a characterization such as invitation–acceptance may oversimplify more subtle, gradual emergences. Another extension of previous findings involves showing how participants extend a moment of shared laughter into a lengthier laughing together. Different methods for doing this – extending laughs themselves, extending laughter for one referent, or creating new laughables – reflect different orientations to emerging situations.

Chapter 4 moves attention from primary focus on structure to the interplay of structure and identity by considering who laughs first and how that proves consequential to displayed orientations and alignments. A statistical distribution shows that commonly in two-party interpersonal interactions, current speaker initiates shared laughter, while in multi-party interpersonal interactions, someone else starts laughing first. Commonly, current speakers produce the laughable utterances or actions. When laughable producers have the opportunity to withhold first laugh they will do so if laughing first might be hearable as self-praise. That opportunity is less present in two-party interactions, for shared laughter cannot occur unless laughable producer participates. Exceptions to this pattern tend to point to other normative orientations, located in the sort of laughable (not all laughables constituting speaker's own material, produced in order to be humorous). "Who laughs first" also shows orientation to activities in which laughables and laughter get embedded, such as issuing and declining invitations.

Chapter 5 considers interplay of structure and participant identity by emphasizing laughter's ability to show affiliation or disaffiliation, characterized as *laughing with* or *laughing at*. *Laughing at* is marked by four keys: a laughable that nominates someone co-present as butt; first laugh by someone else; second laugh not present or done by someone else; and continued talk on topic. *Laughing at* and *with* set into play different interactional environments carrying social and relational consequences. Case studies in Chapter 5 show how *laughing at* may get transformed into *laughing with* and vice versa. It is argued that these provide micro-moments of transforming social structure.

Chapter 6 concerns laughter as complicit in or resisting interactional activities. In the environment of teases and improprieties, shared laughter contributes to sequences leading up to displays of conversational intimacy or play. Teases can be at the expense of the laugher, and improprieties may seek to draw recipient into affiliating with relationship or stance which the recipient might wish to resist. Laughing responsively shows appreciation but by itself only ambiguously affiliates in the offensive or teasing mentality. The laughing along option ratifies treating the referent playfully and serves as a warrant for interactants to produce more of the same, thereby displaying and extending intimacy. In this way, shared laughter plays an important role both in framing play and in marking a relationship as intimate. However, laughter may also show resistance, though less markedly so (or more ambiguously) than would an outright, non-laughing rejection. Two case studies show women laughing along with teases or improprieties from men and yet resisting further development of possibly sexual topics. Because this is consistent with claims of gender-distributed activities, I close the chapter with a discussion of how one might build an empirical argument for participant orientation to gender in the sequential organization of laughter.

The progression of Chapters 2 through 6 moves from basic to applied conversation analysis (ten Have, 1999). Basic CA concerns the explication of features of interaction oriented-to by participants. Applied CA links to interests in how human relationships and contexts get constituted in interaction. Chapters 2 through 4 sustain attention to basic phenomena of sequential organization. In Chapters 5 and 6 attention shifts to how people, through laughter and shared laughter, display, respond to, and negotiate alignment, framing, relationship, and identity. These applied extensions offer bridges to research in related methods and fields such as interpersonal communication (especially relational) and gender and communication.

Chapter 6 answers recent calls in relational communication fields for direct attention to talk-in-interaction as the primary locus of relationship work. Duck (1990) and others in the relational communication field have called for more talk-centered studies of interpersonal relationships. Goldsmith and Baxter (1996) write:

> In addition to thinking of relationships in sociological terms (e.g., casual acquaintances, friends, spouses) and psychological terms (e.g., less intimate, close, distant), scholars might benefit from developing communication-based ways of characterizing relationships that reflect native constructions of relating; for example, "We have the kind of relationship in which you can tell everything," "We have a 'joking around' relationship," "I enjoy shooting the breeze with him, but I'd never talk to him about anything serious," "It seems like all we do is fight anymore," and so forth. (p. 89)

"Relationship" is an abstract concept that researchers operationalize and study in a variety of ways. A constitutive view means treating relationship, not as taken-for-granted or pre-determined, but brought into being by participants through their communicative conduct. In work foundational to the study of relational communication, Gregory Bateson and colleagues of the Palo Alto group (see Watzlawick, Bavelas, and Jackson, 1967) regarded relationship messages as metacommunicative to and part of all communication. According to this thinking, people continually display their definition of relationship with their interlocutor(s) in both subtle and explicit ways. Some would argue that it is misleading to equate talk with relationship (for example, Sigman, 1995, p. 192), for these represent different levels of abstraction. Nevertheless, we have much to learn by treating relationships as communicative accomplishments and examining peoples' methods for constituting them.

Oft-studied in relational communication research, intimacy proves useful as a concept to distinguish close relationships (such as romantic partners or family members), presumed to feature intimacy, to remote ones for which intimacy is not likely to be present. Models of developing relationships show movement from initial interaction as strangers to intimacy as the most unified condition possible. Underlying such models is an assumption that people desire intimacy and attempt to achieve it in and through close relationships. Although it is tempting to equate certain relationship categories (such as married couple) automatically with intimacy, most researchers accept a more fluid treatment which allows for the possibilities that married couples may act at times in highly non-intimate ways and, conversely, that near-strangers may communicate intimately under certain circumstances.

Several recent studies attempt to ground empirically characterizations of relational intimacy. Hopper, Knapp, and Scott (1981) developed the idea that intimate talk is characterized by the use of idioms unique to that relationship. Idiomatic words, phrases, and expressions invoke a private code used to negotiate behavioral norms, promote bonding, and deal with social constraints. Owen (1987) argued for the importance of research linking conversational-level with relational-level phenomena, examining exchanges of "I love you" as adjacency pairs for dating and married couples. Berlyne (1969), Glenn and Knapp (1987), and Baxter (1990) among others have investigated connections between relational intimacy and play. Hopper and Drummond (1990) presented an instance of what they deemed a naturally occurring "turning point" in a relationship, captured in a telephone conversation; in this case, a couple moves markedly from more to less intimate status. Hopper and Drummond (1992) examine systematic structural differences in the phone openings of strangers and intimates. Mandelbaum (1989) shows how people display themselves as members of a couple through the co-telling of stories. She also presents an argument for the "tit for tat" move in conversation being explicitly about relationship (Mandelbaum, 2003). Beach (1996) traces the constitution of a family relationship through a recorded interaction in which a grandmother confronts her granddaughter's eating disorder. Foregrounding explicit connections between relationship and talk, these studies connect to and pave the way for the analysis presented in Chapter 6.

Chapter 6 shows how interactants create displays of relational intimacy through improprieties and teases. Both activities regularly occur in the environment of shared laughter. Shared laughter provides a sequential environment in which it is relevant for speakers to produce additional improprieties or teases. Through mutual uses of impropriety or teasing people display interactional intimacy. Shared laughter is important to the sequential organization and interactional workings of both improprieties and teasing; thus this chapter traces close connections between laughter and intimacy. A third conceptual partner, play, provides a bridge between laughter and intimacy. Shared laughter provides a primary framing for play as a metacommunicative and relational context, and in the pursuit of play conversationalists may display interactional intimacy.

In this analysis I am proposing a conceptual hierarchy, arrayed from micro to macro, from concrete to abstract, from empirically analyzable to inferable, as follows. Laughter, specifically shared laughter, provides a warrant for producing improprieties and teases. These provide ways to display conversational intimacy. They also provide ways to mark a context of play. Intimacy and play are characterizations of relationship (however fleeting). Shared laughter, then, contributes to and provides evidence of intimacy and play in interaction and in relationship. This is not surprising; most people will recognize that laughing together, under the right circumstances, can help us feel close to (intimate with) others.

Relationship is one definition of situation, or one kind of context. How laughter contributes to context gets taken up centrally in the last section of Chapter 6 in an exploration of whether (and how) laughter displays participant orientation to gender. It is argued that laughs reflect, and constitute, different orientations to context. The choice to laugh or not laugh may display acceptance of or resistance to some definition-of-situation proposed by other. Laughs show orientation to context not only by their presence or absence, but also through their acoustic features, length, and sequential placement, all of which contribute to marking laughter's footing in relation to the laughable, the participants, and the situation. Although not possessing linguistic or semantic content, laughs still allow for varied, nuanced, and subtle displays of definitions of situation.

Technology will continue opening up ways to study interaction. In recent years, high quality digital video editing has created possibilities for more subtle and detailed analyses of both aural and visual features of laughter and other features of human interaction (see for example, Jarmon, 1996). Digital sound tracks enable researchers to be more precise in locating onset, development, and termination of laughs. Capturing visual images digitally opens up new possibilities for investigating laughing, smiling, and related activities. Chapter 3 presents a case study intended as a demonstration of the sorts of phenomena such investigations might yield. However, it would be misleading to assume that increased technological sophistication necessarily leads to better research findings. CA's core enterprise involves explicating people's emergent understandings grounded phenomenologically in lived, embodied experience. Researcher-produced transcription and a spectrograph image offer alternative ways to represent laugh sounds visually on the page. Arguably, the spectrograph image is more "precise." However, the transcription is produced by a researcher engaged in close listening and observation, drawing upon resources as a social actor in the world. The researcher is in the research (although in CA this generally doesn't get explicit attention; for a notable exception, blending CA and ethnography, see Moerman, 1988), and that presence is important in achieving interpretations and making them available to others. Digital audio and video represent welcome possibilities for enhancing the development of transcripts and identification of patterns, but they should not detract CA researchers from basic attention to how people produce and make meaningful actions within interaction.

Chapters 5 and 6 suggest opportunities for a critical turn in the analysis of laughter in interaction. By transforming *laughing at* to *laughing with* or vice versa, participants accomplish micro-level transformations of social structure. The fact that laughter can work both affiliatively and with hostility suggests its potential importance in social constructions of power in relationships. Future work could expand on this possibility, responding to Bogen's (1999) call for a critical conversation analysis. Similarly, arguments about gender and laughter in Chapter 6 invite further development of power currencies located in identity categories such as gender.

Teachers and scholars of human communication often wish to translate research findings into practical applications, with "practical application" meaning concrete skills or recommendations that students can learn. How can we apply lessons about the sequential organization of laughter? Is it possible, or even desirable, to teach laughing as a social skill? I am not prepared to argue, based on the research presented in this book, that we should teach people how to laugh differently. Nor can I wholeheartedly endorse any simple assertion that we should all laugh more. Clearly, laughing can help us deal with difficult situations in life with more focus and creativity and with less anxiety. Laughing can help us feel very good physically, mentally, and spiritually. It can serve as a powerful force in bringing people closer together in relationships. Yet that same laughter can be at the expense of someone else and can lead us to be cruel and unsympathetic. Prescription not grounded in details of particular situations could easily err on the side of gross oversimplification and even prove dangerous. In the many hours of interaction I have examined, I often have encountered instances in which I felt people were laughing awkwardly, inappropriately, or ineptly. However, that does not lead me to want to teach people to do it differently. The awkward laugh has its place and accomplishes something; declining a laugh invitation is the right thing to do in some cases. Laughter resists easy formulations. So, I offer no prescriptive advice for particular behaviors. I will only offer the following four recommendations, and each should be treated suspiciously.

Seek out hearty laughter. There now exists enough anecdotal and empirical evidence to take seriously claims of the physiological and psychological benefits of regular, sustained, hearty laughter. Look for such opportunities.

Seek out shared laughter. Treasure those moments when shared laughter gets extended into laughing together, the prolonged bouts of communal hysteria which leave us weak and giddy. These don't solve the world's problems, but they help us sustain healthy mental attitudes and stronger social bonds.

Be aware of the ecology of laughing. Remember that laughter can hurt people. Remember that it can dampen your ability to empathize with others. Be aware that each time you laugh at the expense of another person or group, you may be contributing in a small way to perpetuating a system of domination.

Make sure at least 50% of your laughter is at your own expense. To assign such a percent is ludicrous, but the point is a serious one. Laughing at oneself encourages humility and works against hubris. Done properly, it helps keep egotism in check and reminds us that we are as laughable as other humans. However, it too requires moderation. The goal is to achieve a healthy balance, perceiving oneself as neither consistently superior nor inferior to the rest of humanity. We must understand ourselves as like other people: able to be funny, able to laugh at oneself and others, able to suffer the slings and arrows of life without excessive grimness.

Despite resistance to explicit prescriptive applications, I believe there are important pedagogical connections from this research. These derive, not from telling people what to do, but from inviting people to examine what they do and let them decide what they might like to change. The study of talk-in-interaction, particularly laughter, has had profound effects on my understandings and my own behaviors. I now am much more aware than ever before of laughing moments in talk. I sometimes catch myself laughing out of anxiety or discomfort in ways that do not contribute positively to the situation; I am able to stop and try to figure out what is going on. I love to laugh with others affiliatively, and I have gotten better at helping bring such moments about, through a well-timed remark, a comic noticing, or a first laugh. I am more aware of some laughable moments I wish to resist (a joke that I find offensive, for example); I am more able to resist. I am more aware than ever of the power of laughter to pull participants into relationship definitions and identity displays which may be more or less desirable. I don't always do what I think is best when it comes to laughter, but when I don't I'm far more likely to understand why. Finally, because it is metacommunicative and reframing, laughter (both as practice and subject of study) helps me resist an overly ponderous approach to everyday life and reminds me not to take my doings, or those of any other persons, too seriously. I treasure laughter's spontaneity, quirkiness, and ambiguity; I respect its volatility and danger; I am drawn by its mystery. Although my goal in this book is to provide more comprehensive understandings of laughter in interaction, I hope we never fully get it.

Notes

1 Towards a social interactional approach to laughter

1. This raises the question of whether laughter proves suitable as a single term to refer to so many phenomena that may differ in sight, sound, motivation, and meaning. We make an analytic mistake if we assume a discrete phenomenon simply because a single word covers all manifestations. In English, there are many other words which refer to particular kinds of laughs, but the word "laugh" does seem applicable to all of these. It is the umbrella term, and words like "giggle" and "chortle" seem to invoke subsets. Informal data gathered from a convenience sample of other languages (Russian, French, German, Romanian, Azerbaijani, Chinese, and Japanese) suggest that they all possess a word or concept which covers roughly the same domain as "laugh." With the exception of Chinese, in all these languages the word "laugh" excludes smiling. It seems that across diverse languages and cultures people constitute laughing as a unitary construct, despite variation within the category. At this point, there does not seem to be evidence for a case against using laughter as a general category. (Thanks to Alex Kozin for helping collect information from other languages.)

2. Less plausible are claims that dogs and dolphins smile and laugh. The dolphin's "smile" reflects the upward curve of the mouth line. The dog's "laugh" often accompanies panting and occurs in a friendly context. Both species can be extremely playful among their own kinds as well as with humans. However, the resemblance of these facial expressions to human or primate smiles or laughs seems merely coincidental.

3. Consider the following sample of items. An employee newsletter at a major US university encourages readers to laugh and play in order to enhance their physical and mental health. An article in *Psychology Today* (Doskoch, 1996) discusses the positive physical and psychological benefits of laughter and advocates developing the inclination to laugh. Similar articles have appeared recently in such publications as *RN* for nurses (McGhee, 1998) and *American Behavioral Scientist* (Solomon, 1996). Dr. Joel Goodman, director of the HUMOR project, holds

annual conferences devoted to exploring the healing power of humor and laughter. *American Health Magazine* (Lang, 1988) reports that such corporations as IBM, Bell Telephone, Monsanto, General Foods, and Hartford Insurance Group have made explicit attempts to introduce humor to enhance the workplace in the belief that this will help improve employee creativity, decision-making, and negotiating abilities. Several web sites continue developing similar ideas (for example, www.aath.org; www.humorproject.com; and www.intopnet/-jrdunn/). A popular 1998 film based on the life of Dr. Hunter "Patch"Adams follows the story of an idealistic physician who actively encourages humor, laughter, and play as part of the healing environment for his patients. Clifford Kuhn, M.D., Clinical Professor of Psychiatry at the University of Louisville School of Medicine, took a sabbatical to tour as a stand-up comedian in order to study humor and healing. He now brings these notions into his work with cancer patients. Kuhn and comedian Jerry Lewis offer humor workshops for other doctors (Barry, 1999). Sutorius (1995) advocates "laughing meditation" as a way to put the "transforming force of laughter" to work for psychological counseling patients. Roustang (1987) makes the case that in psychotherapy, client laughter implies an ability not to take the world seriously and thus opens up the possibility for therapeutic change; in contrast, the inability to laugh is symptomatic of paranoia.

4. Interestingly, the genre of "dumb blonde jokes" generally makes fun of blonde females, but my daughter Kristin (who was twelve at the time) told me this joke with "he" being the stupid one. Apparently, the dumb blond stereotype can carry across gender.

5. Indeed, there have been rare cases of group hysterical laughter, sometimes lasting for days (Stearns, 1972, pp. 40–43; Provine, 2000, pp. 129–133). In regard to these cases, the prevailing explanation is that laughter proves "contagious" to such an extreme that large groups of people cannot stop themselves for laughing until they grow weak.

3 Laughing together

1. It may be that the physician smiles or otherwise indicates playfulness visually but not aurally. See discussion beginning on p. 66.

2. Adelsward (1989) critiques Jefferson's research for treating all first laughs as invitations to shared laughter. As the preceding discussion shows, this is clearly not the case.

3. Based on data from a case study of Algonquin conversation, Spielman (1988) argues that a bid to extend shared laughter may fail if it offers no new laughable or additional information.

4 Who laughs first

1. There are various ways to conceptualize the "who" question, for example through the roles often used to distinguish among people: class, race,

sex, marital status, relationship to other, etc. In exploring "who laughs first?" we might wonder whether children laugh first, or funny people, or more educated people, or women, and so forth. Indeed, some have suggested that women are more likely to laugh at men's jokes than vice versa (Provine, 1993; also see p. 150 above). No ways of characterizing "who" are neutral; all reflect ideology and choice. In everyday communication, we invoke individual identities through labels fitted to particular interlocutors and particular moments in interaction. Likewise, social science research categories are products of choices researchers make. The treatment of "who" in this chapter remains grounded in details of talk and focuses on the sequential roles of current speaker and other(s), and laughable-producer and other(s). How such changeable roles might align with other contextual roles, such as gender or relationship, draws increasing attention in the analyses in Chapters 5 and 6.

2. Adelsward (1989) conducted a coding study utilizing three criteria for assessing who issues a laugh invitation: institutional role (such as interviewer), formal or temporal (grounded in turn structure), or pragmatic (who produces the laughable).

3. Violations of this rule themselves provide a basis for laughs. Early in his career, the American comedian Steve Martin would sometimes tell a deliberately stupid joke then immediately produce loud, overdone laughter. This combination drew laughter from the audience. For further contrasting of expectations for speaker laughter between public comedy and casual talk settings, see Muller, 1992.

4. Nancy may provide an example in conversation of what in theatrical contexts is known as a *shill*. Recognizing that social cues influence people's appreciation of performances (and displays of such appreciation), vaudeville theaters or performers would sometimes hire audience member(s) to applaud, thus stimulating the rest of the audience to join in, creating the impression of a more successful performance. A similar motivation underlies the use in television of laugh tracks, live studio audiences, and signs instructing such audiences to applaud. Goffman (1959, pp. 146–147) compares conversational with theatrical shills:

> A shill is someone who acts as though he were an ordinary member of the audience but is in fact in league with the performers. Typically, the shill either provides a visible model for the audience of the kind of response the performers are seeking or provides the kind of audience response that is necessary at the moment for the development of the performance. The designation "shill" and "claque," employed in the entertainment business, have come into common use. . . . We must not take the view that shills are found only in non-respectable performances. . . . For example, at informal conversational gatherings, it is common for a wife to look interested when her husband tells an anecdote and to feed him appropriate leads and cues, although in fact she has heard the anecdote many times and knows that the show her husband is making of telling something for the first time is only a show.

A shill can display that laughter is appropriate and invite laughter from others. As Goffman points out, members of a couple may share experiences or knowledge that enable them to act as shills for each other. This does not necessarily imply dishonest collusion or prior planning. It does point out that, in multi-party interactions, people may assume separate roles of laughable-producer, laugh-shill, and respondents.

5. These excerpts reflect a different numbering system. Line numbers begin anew at the top of each page of the entire Rah transcript. Thus, when I indicate the first line of an excerpt as "21:4" that means I am beginning with line 4 on page 21 of the original.

5 *Laughing at* and *laughing with*

1. In fact, Vaughn may not be the only one who fails to get the joke on first telling. Out of the entire group, only Chris and Cecil explicitly demonstrate understanding through laughter and appreciative comments. Display of one participant's understanding failure foregrounds the relevance for others to display that they *do* get it. In such an environment, an absence of positive understanding cues – note, for example, Ethel's silence – may serve as stronger evidence of failure to get. (My thanks to Gail Jefferson for this observation.)

6 Laughing along, resisting

1. Rick's laugh responsive to Cara's original error seems clearly laughing at her. Her own introduction of additional laughable error-forms may be a means of attempting to get him to laugh with her. In the lines above, Cara may shift orientation to being laughed at as part of her movement away from the series of escalating error-laughables.

2. Here an interesting twist occurs. Rick's "bad" form of the verb *go* (line 529) is *really* bad – that is, his variant, combining the long *o* of *go* with a terminal *un* sound, is not recognizably a legitimate verb form at all. Thus it does not follow the rules of the distortion-game as they have been playing it up to now, by providing real, though inappropriate, versions of action verbs. Cara displays awareness that this is not a "proper" error. She initiates repair containing a real (and "properly" incorrect) verb form, "gone" (line 531). Rick accepts this repair by repeating it. The "wrong" version now corrected, Cara and Rick laugh together in appreciation of the error (lines 532 and 533).

3. Withholding laughter also can accomplish resistance (see Chapter 3 on declined laugh invitations). In the example below, Ida reports some bit of speech and laughs while saying "hurt yourself." Jenny does not laugh but immediately following the second laugh particle asks a question.

(Rah:II:10)

10	IDA	=cz -(ih) se t ah:'ll pop round if yiv
11		heu:rtchise(h)e(h) lf (or someth' •hh)
12	JENNY	⌈What ti:me d 'e ⌉ri ng.

Talking rather than laughing provides a way to disattend laughable features of the referent and thereby perhaps to resist participating in an activity in which the laughable plays a part.

4. Not only is it what callers commonly do, if a caller does offer last name the hosts sometimes will explicitly admonish against that practice. See also Chandler's statement of the rule, lines 14–16.

5. The upward intonation is slight; in earlier versions of the transcript, I did not indicate it.

6. Interestingly, though, the remainder of the interaction contains several words or phrases which have markedly sexual meanings. It may be that this environment has been "fertilized" for such possibilities. (See Jefferson, 1994)

References

Adams, R. M., and Kirkevold, B. (1977). *Looking, smiling, laughing, and moving in restaurants: sex and age differences*. EDRS publication. New York: Human Sciences Press.

Adelsward, Viveka (1989). Laughter and dialogue: the social significance of laughter in institutional discourse. *Nordic Journal of Linguistics* 12: 2, 107–136.

Armstrong, S. A. (1992). Teasables, teases, and responses in conversational teasing sequences. Unpublished master's thesis, Southern Illinois University Carbondale.

Askenasy, J. J. M. (1987). The functions and dysfunctions of laughter. *Journal of General Psychology* 114: 4, 317–334.

Atkinson, J. M., and Heritage, J. (eds.) (1984). *Structures of social action: Studies in conversation analysis*. Cambridge: Cambridge University Press.

Avery, C., and Antaki, C. (1997). Conversational devices in stories turning on appearance versus reality. *Text* 17, 1–24.

Bailey, J. (1976). *Intent on laughter*. New York: Quadrangle.

Bakhtin, M. (1968). *Rabelais and his world* (trans. H. Iswolsky). Cambridge, MA: MIT Press.

Bales, R. F. (1950). *Interaction process analysis; a method for the study of small groups*. Cambridge, MA: Addison-Wesley.

Barry, P. (1999). It's no joke; humor heals, *AARP Magazine* (April), 14–17.

Basso, K. (1979). *Portraits of "the Whiteman"; linguistic play and cultural symbols among the Western Apache*. Cambridge: Cambridge University Press.

Bateson, G. (1972). A theory of play and fantasy. In *Steps to an ecology of mind* (pp. 177–193). New York: Ballantine.

Bavelas, J. B. (1995). Quantitative vs. qualitative? In W. Leeds-Hurwitz (ed.), *Social approaches to communication* (pp. 49–62). New York: Guilford.

Baxter, L. A. (1990). Intimate play in friendships and romantic relationships. Paper presented to the Speech Communication Association annual meeting, Chicago. (November.)

Beach, W. A. (1996). *Conversations about illness; family preoccupations with bulimia*. Mahwah, NJ: Lawrence Erlbaum Associates.

Beach, W. A. and Dixson, C. N. (2000). Revealing moments: Formulating understandings of adverse experiences in a health appraisal interview. *Social Science and Medicine, 52*, 25–45.

Berlyne, D. E. (1969). Laughter, humor, and play. In G. Lindzey and E. Aronson (eds.), *The handbook of social psychology* (2nd edn., pp. 795–852). Reading, MA: Addison-Wesley.

Black, D. W. (1984). Laughter. *Journal of the American Medical Association* 252, 2995–2998.

Bogen, D. (1999). *Order without rules; critical theory and the logic of conversation*. Albany: SUNY Press.

Bormann, E. G. (1981). Fantasy and rhetorical vision; rhetorical criticism of social reality. In J. F. Cragan and D. C. Shields (eds.), *Applied communication research: a dramatistic approach* (pp. 15–29). Prospect Heights, IL; Waveland Press.

Brown, G. E., Brown, D., Ramos, J. (1981). Effects of a laughing versus a nonlaughing model on humor response in college students. *Psychological Reports* 48, 35–40.

Camras, L. A., Malatesta, C., and Izard, C. E. (1991). The development of facial expressions in infancy. In R. S. Feldman and B. Rime (eds.), *Fundamentals of nonverbal behavior* (pp. 73–105). Cambridge: Cambridge University Press.

Chapman, A. J. (1976). Social aspects of humorous laughter. In A. J. Chapman and H. C. Foot (eds.), *Humour and laughter; theory, research and applications* (pp. 155–185). London: John Wiley and Sons.

Clayman, S. E. (1992). Caveat orator: audience disaffiliation in the 1988 presidential debates. *Quarterly Journal of Speech* 78, 33–60.

Coser, R. L. (1960). Laughter among colleagues; a study of the social functions of humor among the staff of a mental hospital. *Psychiatry* 23, 81–95.

Cousins, N. (1979). *Anatomy of an illness as perceived by the patient*. New York: Norton.

Cox, M. (1982). Regularities in the content of statements "Said with a Laugh." Paper presented at the American Psychological Association Meeting, Washington DC. (ERIC document ED222963.) (August.)

Crow, B. K. (1986). Conversational pragmatics in television talk: the discourse of *Good Sex*. *Media, Culture, and Society* 8, 457–484.

Darwin, C. R. (1872/1955). *The expression of the emotions in man and animals*. New York: Philosophical Society.

Davies, C. E. (1985). Joint joking: improvisational humorous episodes in conversation. In D. L. F. Nilsen and A. P. Nilsen (eds.), *Whimsy III: contemporary humor (Proceedings of the 1984 WHIM Conference)* (pp. 133–134). English Department, Arizona State University.

Doskoch, P. (1996). Happily ever after: psychological benefits of laughter. *Psychology Today* 29, 32–34.

Drew, P. (1987). Po-faced receipts of teases. *Linguistics* 25, 219–253.

Duchowny, M. S. (1983). Pathological disorders of laughter. In P. E. McGhee and J. H. Goldstein (eds.), *Handbook of humor research*. Volume 2: Applied studies (pp. 88–108). New York: Springer-Verlag.

Duck, S. W. (1990). Relationships as unfinished business: out of the frying pan and into the 1990s. *Journal of Social and Personal Relationships* 7, 5–29.

Edmondson, Munro S. (1987). Notes on laughter. *Anthropological Linguistics* 29, 23–34.

Eibl-Eibesfeldt, I. (1989). *Human ethology.* New York: Aldine De Gruyter.

Emerson, Joan (1973). Negotiating the serious import of humor. In A. Birenbaum and E. Sagarin (eds.), *People in places: the sociology of the familiar* (pp. 269–280). London: Nelson.

Falk, Dana R., and Hill, C. E. (1992). Counselor interventions preceding client laughter in brief therapy. *Journal of Counseling Psychology* 39, 39–45.

Fogel, A., Dickson, K. L., Hsu, H., Messinger, D., Nelson-Goens, G. C., and Nwokah, E. (1997). Communication of smiling and laughter in mother-infant play: research on emotion from a dynamic systems perspective. *New Directions for Child Development* 77, 5–23.

Foot, H. C. (1997). Humour and laughter. In O. D. W. Hargie (ed.), *The handbook of communication skills* (2nd edn.) (pp. 259–288). London and New York: Routledge.

Foot, H. C., and Chapman, A. J. (1976). The social responsiveness of young children in humorous situations. In A. J. Chapman and H. C. Foot (eds.), *Humour and laughter; theory, research and applications* (pp. 187–214). London: John Wiley and Sons.

Freedman, J. L., and Perlick, D. (1979). Crowding, contagion, and laughter. *Journal of Experimental Social Psychology* 15, 295–303.

Freud, S. (1938). Wit and its relation to the unconscious. In A. A. Brill (ed. and trans.) *The basic writings of Sigmund Freud* (pp. 631–805). New York: Modern Library.

Fry, W. F. (1977). The appeasement function of mirthful laughter. In A. J. Chapman and H. C. Foot (eds.), *It's a funny thing, humour* (pp. 23–26). Oxford: Pergamon.

Fry, W. F., and Allen, M. (1975). *Make 'em laugh.* Palo Alto, CA: Science and Behavior Books.

Garfinkel, H. (1967). *Studies in ethnomethodology.* Englewood Cliffs, NJ: Prentice Hall.

Glenn, P. J. (1987). Laugh and the world laughs with you; shared laughter sequencing in conversation. Unpublished doctoral dissertation, University of Texas at Austin.

(1989). Initiating shared laughter in multi-party conversations. *Western Journal of Speech Communication* 53: 2, 127–149.

(1989a). Some techniques for extending conversational shared laughter. Paper presented at the Speech Comunication Association, San Francisco. (November.)

(1990). Shared laughter, intimacy, and play. Paper presented at the Speech Communication Association Convention, Chicago.

(1992). Current speaker initiation of two-party shared laughter. *Research on Language and Social Interaction* 25, 139–162.

(1995). Laughing at and laughing with: negotiating participant alignments through conversational laughter. In P. ten Have and G. Psathas (eds.), *Situated order: studies in the social organization of talk and embodied activities* (pp. 43–56). Lanham, MD: University Press of America.

(2000). Sex, laughter, and audiotape: the laughter-gender connection. Paper presented at the International Pragmatics Association Conference, Budapest, Hungary. (July.)

(2003). Sex, laughter, and audiotape: On invoking features of context to explain laughter in interaction. In P. J. Glenn, C. D. LeBaron, and J. Mandelbaum (eds.), *Studies in Language and Social Interaction* (pp. 265–276). Lawrence Erlbaum & Associates.

Glenn, P. J., and Knapp, M. L. (1987). The interactive framing of play in adult conversations. *Communication Quarterly*, 35, 48–66.

Glenn, P. J., Hoffman, E., and Hopper, R. (1996). Woman, laughter, man: gender and the sequential organization of laughter. Paper presented at the American Association of Applied Linguistics Convention, Chicago. (March.)

Goffman, E. (1959). *The presentation of self in everyday life*. Garden City, NY: Doubleday Anchor Books.

(1974). *Frame analysis; an essay on the organization of experience*. New York: Harper & Row.

Goldsmith, D. J., and Baxter, L. A. (1996). Constituting relationships in talk; a taxonomy of speech events in social and personal relationships. *Human Communication Research* 23, 87–114.

Goldstein, J. H., and McGhee, P. E. (eds.). (1972). *The psychology of humor; Theoretical perspectives and empirical issues*. New York: Academic Press.

Goodwin, C. (1979). The interactive construction of a sentence in natural conversation. In G. Psathas (ed.), *Everyday language; studies in ethnomethodology* (pp. 23–78). New York: Irvington.

(1984). Notes on story structure and the organization of participation. In J. M. Atkinson and J. Heritage (eds.), *Structures of social action: studies in conversation analysis* (pp. 225–246). Cambridge: Cambridge University Press.

Gray, J. (1992). *Men are from Mars, women are from Venus: a practical guide for improving communication and getting what you want in relationships*. New York: HarperCollins.

Gregory, D. (1964). *Nigger: an autobiography*. New York: Dutton.

Gregory, J. C. (1924). *The nature of laughter*. London: Kegan Paul.

Gruner, C. R. (1978). *Understanding laughter: the workings of wit and humor*. Chicago: Nelson-Hall.

Haakana, M. (1999). Laughing matters; a conversation analytical study of laughter in doctor-patient interaction. Unpublished doctoral dissertation, Department of Finnish Language, University of Helsinki.

Hayworth, D. (1928). The social origin and function of laughter. *Psychological Review* 35, 367–384.

Heath, C. (1984). Talk and recipiency; Sequential organization in speech and body movement. In J. M. Atkinson and J. Heritage (eds.), *Structures of social action: studies in conversation analysis* (pp. 247–265). Cambridge: Cambridge University Press.

Heritage, J. (1984). A change-of-state token and aspects of its sequential placement. In J. M. Atkinson and J. Heritage (eds.), *Structures of social action: studies in conversation analysis* (pp. 299–345). Cambridge: Cambridge University Press.

Heritage, J., and Atkinson, J. M. (1984). Transcript notation. In J. M. Atkinson and J. Heritage (eds.), *Structures of social action: studies in conversation analysis* (pp. ix–xvi). Cambridge: Cambridge University Press.

Hertzler, J. O. (1970). *Laughter; a socio-scientific analysis*. New York: Exposition Press.

Holland, N. N. (1982). *Laughing; a psychology of humor*. Ithaca, NY: Cornell University Press.

Hopper, R. (1992). *Telephone conversation*. Bloomington: Indiana University Press.

   (2002). *Gendering talk*. East Lansing: Michigan State University Press.

Hopper, R., and Drummond, K. (1990). Emergent goals at a relational turning point: the case of Gordon and Denise. *Journal of Language and Social Psychology* 9, 39–65.

   (1992). Accomplishing interpersonal relationship: telephone openings of strangers and intimates. *Western Journal of Speech Communication* 3, 185–200.

Hopper, R., and Glenn, P. J. (1994). Repetition and play in conversation. In B. Johnstone (ed.), *Repetition in discourse: interdisciplinary perspectives* (vol. II) (pp. 29–40). Norwood, NJ: Ablex.

Hopper, R., and LeBaron, C. (1998). How gender creeps into talk. *Research on Language and Social Interaction* 31: 1, 59–74.

Hopper, R., Knapp, M. L., and Scott, L. (1981). Couples' personal idioms: exploring intimate talk. *Journal of Communication* 31, 23–33.

Jarmon, L. H. (1996). An ecology of embodied interaction. Unpublished doctoral dissertation (available on compact disc), University of Texas at Austin.

Jefferson, G. (n.d.) Some features of the serial construction of laughter. Unpublished manuscript, University of Massachusetts, Amherst.

(1972). Side sequences. In D. Sudnow (ed.), *Studies in social interaction* (pp. 294–338). New York: Free Press.

(1974). Notes on the sequential organization of laughter in conversation; onset sensitivity in invitations to laugh. Paper presented at the American Anthropological Association Convention, Mexico City.

Jefferson, G. (1979). A technique for inviting laughter and its subsequent acceptance declination. In G. Psathas (ed.), *Everyday language: studies in ethnomethodology* (pp. 79–96). New York: Irvington.

(1984). On the organization of laughter in talk about troubles. In J. M. Atkinson and J. Heritage (eds.), *Structures of social action: studies in conversation analysis* (pp. 346–369). Cambridge: Cambridge University Press.

(1985). An exercise in the transcription and analysis of laughter. In T. A. van Dijk (ed.), *Handbook of discourse analysis; Volume 3: Discourse and dialogue* (pp. 25–34). London: Academic Press.

(1994). A note on laughter in 'Male-Female' interaction. Unpublished manuscript. (May.)

Jefferson, G., Sacks, H., and Schegloff, E. (1977). *Preliminary notes on the sequential organization of laughter.* (Pragmatics Microfiche). Cambridge: Cambridge University, Department of Linguistics.

(1987). Notes on laughter in the pursuit of intimacy. In G. Button and J. R. E. Lee (eds.), *Talk and social organisation* (pp. 152–205). Clevedon: Multilingual Matters.

Kant, I. (1790/1952). *The critique of judgment.* Trans. by J. Meredith. Oxford: Clarendon.

Koestler, A. (1964). *The act of creation.* London: Hutchinson.

LaFrance, M. (1983). Felt vs. feigned funniness: issues in coding smiling and laughing. In P. E. McGhee and J. H. Goldstein (eds.), *Handbook of Humor Research.* vol. 1: *Basic Issues* (pp. 1–12). New York: Springer-Verlag.

LaFrance, M., and Hecht, M. A. (1999). Option or obligation to smile: the effects of power and gender on facial expression. In P. Philippot, R. S. Feldman, and E. J. Coats (eds.), *The Social context of nonverbal behavior* (pp. 45–70). Cambridge: Cambridge University Press.

Lang, S. (1988). Laughing matters at work. *American Health* 46. (September.)

Lavin, D., and Maynard, D. W. (1998). Standardization vs. rapport: how interviewers handle the laughter of respondents during telephone surveys. Unpublished manuscript, University of Indiana.

LeBaron, C. D., Mandelbaum, J., and Glenn, P. J. (2003). An overview of language and social interaction research. In P. J. Glenn, C. D. LeBaron, and J. Mandelbaum (eds.), *Studies in language and social interaction* (pp. 1–39). Lawrence Erlbaum and Associates.

Leopold, N. A. (1977). Gaze-induced laughter. *Journal of Neurology, Neurosurgery, and Psychiatry* 40, 815–817.

Lerner, G. H. (1989). Notes on overlap management in conversation: the case of delayed completion. *Western Journal of Speech Communication* 53, 167–77.

Levinson, S. C. (1983). *Pragmatics*. Cambridge: Cambridge University Press.

Lippert, L. (1998). Declined invitations to shared laughter in conversation: a conversation analytic exploration. Paper presented at the National Communication Association Convention, New York. (November.)

Loizos, C. (1967). Play in higher primates: a review. In D. Morris (ed.), *Primate ethology* (pp. 176–218). Chicago, IL: Aldine.

Ludovici, A. M. (1932). *The secret of laughter*. London: Constable.

Mallett, J., and A'Hern, R. (1996). Comparative distribution and use of humour within nurse-patient communication. *International Journal of Nursing Sudies* 33: 5, 530–550.

Mandelbaum, J. (1989). Interpersonal activities in conversational story-telling. *Western Journal of Speech Communication* 53, 114–126.

    (2003). Interactive methods for constructing relationships. In P. J. Glenn, C. D. LeBaron, and J. Mandelbaum (eds.), *Studies in language and social interaction* (pp. 209–222). Lawrence Erlbaum and Associates.

Martin, G. N., and Gray, C. D. (1996). The effects of audience laughter on men's and women's responses to humor. *The Journal of Social Psychology* 136, 221–231.

Maynard, D. W. (1997). The news delivery sequence: bad news and good news in conversational interaction. *Research on Language and Social Interaction* 30, 93–130.

McGhee, P. (1998). Rx; Laughter. *RN* 61, 50–53.

Milford, P. A. (1977). The functions of laughter as human communication. Unpublished master's thesis, Eastern Michigan University, Ypsilanti.

    (1980). Perception of laughter and its acoustical properties. Unpublished doctoral dissertation, Pennsylvania State University, College Park. Abstract in 1981 Dissertation Abstracts International, 41A, 3779A.

Moerman, M. (1988). *Talking culture; ethnography and conversation analysis*. Philadelphia, PA: University of Pennsylvania Press.

Monro, D. H. (1963). *Argument of laughter*. South Bend, IN: University of Notre Dame Press.

Morreall, J. (1983). *Taking laughter seriously*. Albany, NY: State University of New York.

Mowrer, D. E., La Pointe, L. L., and Case, J. L. (1987). Analysis of five acoustic correlates of laughter. *Journal of Nonverbal Behavior* 11, 191–199.

Mulkay, Michael (1988). *On humor; its nature and its place in modern society*. Cambridge: Polity.

Muller, K. (1992). Theatrical moments; on contextualizing funny and dra-
  matic moods in the course of telling a story in conversation. In
  P. Auer and A. Di Luzio (eds.), *The Contextualization of Language*
  (pp. 99–221). Amsterdam: John Benjamins.
Murray, J. A., Bradley, H., Craigie, W. A., and Onions, C. T. (eds.) (1933).
  The Oxford English Dictionary. Volume 6: L-M. Oxford: Clarendon
  Press.
Neuendorf, K. A., and Fennell, T. (1988). A social facilitation view of the
  generation of humor and mirth reactions: effects of a laugh track.
  Central States Speech Journal 39, 37–48.
Norrick, Neal R. (1993). *Conversational joking; humor in everyday talk.*
  Bloomington, IN: Indiana University Press.
O'Donnell-Trujillo, N., and Adams, K. (1983). *Heheh* in conversation: some
  coordinating accomplishments of laughter. *Western Journal of Speech
  Communication* 47, 175–191.
Osborne, K., and Chapman, A. J. (1977). Suppression of adult laughter: an
  experimental approach. In A. J. Chapman and H. C. Foot (eds.), *It's
  a funny thing, humour* (pp. 429–431). Oxford: Pergamon.
Owen, W. F. (1987). Mutual interaction of discourse structures and re-
  lational pragmatics in conversational influence attempts. *Southern
  Speech Communication Journal* 52, 103–127.
Pollio, H. R., and Edgerly, J. W. (1976). Comedians and comic style. In
  A. J. Chapman and H. C. Foot (eds.), *Humour and laughter; theory,
  research and applications* (pp. 215–242). London: John Wiley and
  Sons.
Pollio, H. R., Mers, R., and Lucchesi, W. (1972). Humor, laughter, and
  smiling: some preliminary observations of funny behavior. In J. H.
  Goldstein and P. E. McGhee (eds.), *The psychology of humor; theoretical perspectives and empirical issues* (pp. 211–239). New York:
  Academic Press.
Pomerantz, A. (1980). Telling my side: "limited access" as a "fishing" device. *Sociological Inquiry* 50, 186–198.
  (1984). Agreeing and disagreeing with assessments: some features of
  preferred/dispreferred turn shapes. In J. M. Atkinson and J. Heritage
  (eds.), *Structures of social action: studies in conversation analysis*
  (pp. 247–265). Cambridge: Cambridge University Press.
  (1988). Offering a candidate answer: an information seeking strategy.
  Communication Monographs 55, 360–373.
Provine, Robert R. (1992). Contagious laughter: laughter is a sufficient
  stimulus for laughs and smiles. *Bulletin of the Psychonomic Society*
  30, 1–4.
  (1993). Laughter punctuates speech: linguistic, social and gender contexts
  of laughter. *Ethology* 95, 291–298.
  (2000). *Laughter; a scientific investigation*. New York: Viking.
Provine, R. R., and Yong, Y. L. (1991). Laughter: a Stereotyped human
  vocalization. *Ethology* 89, 115–124.

Psathas, G. (1995). *Conversation analysis; the study of talk-in-interaction.* Thousand Oaks, CA: Sage.

Ragan, S. L. (1990). Verbal play and multiple goals in the gynecologic exam interaction. *Journal of Language and Social Psychology* 9, 67–84.

Raskin, V. (1985). *Semantic mechanisms of humor.* Dordrecht and Boston: Reidel.

Robinson, V. M. (1983). Humor and health. In P. E. McGhee and J. H. Goldstein (eds.), *Handbook of Humor Research.* Volume 2: Applied Studies (pp. 109–128). New York: Springer-Verlag.

Rosenbaum, R. (1978). Kanned Laffter. In J. Monaco (ed.), *Media Culture* (pp. 133–141). New York: Delta Books.

Roustang, F. (1987). How do you make a paranoiac laugh? *MLN* 102: 4, 707–718.

Sacks, H. (1974). An analysis of the course of a joke's telling in conversation. In R. Bauman and J. Sherzer (eds.), *Explorations in the ethnography of speaking* (pp. 337–353). London: Cambridge University Press.

(1984). Notes on methodology. In J. M. Atkinson and J. Heritage (eds.), *Structures of social action: studies in conversation analysis* (pp. 21–27). Cambridge: Cambridge University Press.

Sacks, H. (1992). *Lectures on conversation* (2 vols., G. Jefferson (ed.), with an introduction by E. A. Schegloff). Oxford: Blackwell.

Sacks, H., Schegloff, E. A., and Jefferson, G. (1974). A simplest systematics for the organization of turn-taking in conversation. *Language* 50, 696–735.

Schegloff, E. A. (1979). Identification and recognition in telephone conversation openings. In G. Psathas (ed.), *Everyday language; studies in ethnomethodology* (pp. 23–78). New York: Irvington.

(1984). On some gestures' relation to talk. In J. M. Atkinson and J. Heritage (eds.), *Structures of social action: studies in conversation analysis* (pp. 266–296). Cambridge: Cambridge University Press.

(1992). In another context. In A. Duranti and C. Goodwin (eds.), *Rethinking context: language as an interactive phenomenon* (pp. 191–228). Cambridge: Cambridge University Press.

(1993). Reflections on quantification in the study of conversation. *Research on Language and Social Interaction* 26: 1, 99–128.

Schegloff, E. A. and Sacks, H. (1984). Opening up closings. In J. Baugh and J. Sherzer (eds.), *Language in use: readings in sociolinguistics* (pp. 69–99). Englewood Cliffs, NJ: Prentice-Hall.

Schegloff, E. A., Jefferson, G., and Sacks, H. (1977). The preference for self-correction in the organization of repair in conversation. *Language* 53, 361–382.

Schenkein, J. N. (1972). Towards an analysis of natural conversation and the sense of *heheh. Semiotica* 6, 344–377.

Sigman, S. J. (1995). Order and continuity in human relationships: a social communication approach. In W. Leeds-Hurwitz (ed.), *Social approaches to communication* (pp. 188–200). New York: Guilford.

Simmons-Mackie, N. (2001). Humor in therapy for aphasia. Paper presented at the 7th annual Language and Social Interaction in Communication Disorders Roundtable, University of Rhode Island. (October.)

Solomon, J. (1996). Humor and aging well: a laughing matter or a matter of laughing. *American Behavioral Scientist* 39, 249–272.

Sousa, R. de (1987). *The rationality of emotion*. Cambridge, MA: MIT Press.

Spielman, R. (1988). What's so funny? Laughing together in Algonquin conversation. In William Cowan (ed.), *Papers of the Nineteenth Algonquian Conference* (pp. 201–212). Ottawa: Carleton University.

Stearns, F. R. (1972). *Laughing: physiology, pathophysiology, psychology, pathopsychology, and development*. Springfield, IL: Charles C. Thomas.

Sutorius, D. (1995). The transforming force of laughter, with the focus on the laughing meditation. *Patient Education and Counseling* 26, 367–371. Secretary of the Centre in Favour of Laughter, Jupiter 1007, NL-1115 TX Duivendrecht, The Netherlands.

Tannen, D. (1990). *You just don't understand; women and men in conversation*. New York: William Morrow.

Tracy, K. (1998). Analyzing context: framing the discussion. *Research on Language and Social Interaction* 31: 1, 1–28.

ten Have, P. (1999). *Doing conversation analysis; a practical guide*. London: Sage.

Van Hoof, J. A. R. A. M. (1972). A comparative approach to the phylogeny of laughter and smiling. In R. A. Hinde (ed.), *Non-verbal communication* (pp. 209–241). Cambridge: Cambridge University Press.

Wagner, H., and Lee, V. (1999). Facial behavior alone and in the presence of others. In P. Philippot, R. S. Feldman, and E. J. Coats (eds.), *The social context of nonverbal behavior* (pp. 262–286). Cambridge: Cambridge University Press.

Watzlawick, P., Bavelas, J., and Jackson, D. (1967). *Pragmatics of human communication*. New York: Norton.

Weeks, Mark. (1987). The indifferance in laughter. *MLN* 102: 4, 731–755.

West, C. (1995). Women's competence in conversation. *Discourse and Society* 6, 107–131.

Wilcox, E. W. (1888). Solitude. In *Poems of passion* (p. 131). Chicago, IL: Belford, Clarke, and Co.

Wodak, R. (1997). Introduction: some important issues in the research of gender and discourse. In R. Wodak (ed.), *Gender and Discourse* (pp. 1–20). Thousand Oaks and London: Sage.

Wood, J. T. (1996). She says/he says: communication, caring, and conflict in heterosexual relationships. In J. T. Wood (ed.), *Gendered relationships* (pp. 149–162). Mountain View, CA: Mayfield.

Wright, J. (1990). Free Speech; safe speech is all that's free today. Editorial printed in *The Southern Illinoisan*, September 20th.

Wrobbel, E. D. (1991). Putting the "Punch" in Punchlines. Paper presented at the International Society for Humor Studies Conference, Ontario, Canada. (June.)

Yoon, C. K. (3 June 1997). Anatomy of a tickle is serious business at the research lab. *The New York Times*, B10.

Yoshino, S., Fujimori, J., and Koda, M. (1996). Effects of mirthful laughter on neuroendocrine and immune systems in patients with rheumatoid arthritis. *The Journal of Rheumatology* 23: 4, 793–794.

Zijderveld, A. C. (1983). The sociology of humour and laughter. *Current Sociology* 31, 1–101.

Znaniecki, F. (1934). *The method of sociology*. New York: Farrar and Rinehart.

Index